Sheila Rae

WHY THEY STAY SILENT

AUSTIN MACAULEY PUBLISHERS™
LONDON * CAMBRIDGE * NEW YORK * SHARJAH

Copyright © Sheila Rae (2020)

All rights reserved. No part of this publication may be reproduced, distributed, or transmitted in any form or by any means, including photocopying, recording, or other electronic or mechanical methods, without the prior written permission of the publisher, except in the case of brief quotations embodied in critical reviews and certain other noncommercial uses permitted by copyright law. For permission requests, write to the publisher.

Any person who commits any unauthorized act in relation to this publication may be liable to criminal prosecution and civil claims for damages.

Ordering Information
Quantity sales: special discounts are available on quantity purchases by corporations, associations, and others. For details, contact the publisher at the address below.

Publisher's Cataloging-in-Publication data
Rae, Sheila
Why They Stay Silent

ISBN 9781643783284 (Paperback)
ISBN 9781641828987 (Hardback)
ISBN 9781643785042 (ePub e-book)

www.austinmacauley.com/us

First Published (2021)
Austin Macauley Publishers LLC
40 Wall Street, 33rd Floor, Suite 3302
New York, NY 10005
USA

mail-usa@austinmacauley.com
+1 (646) 5125767

Prologue

The Past

She's been told that her scars depict her past; she's also been told those scars don't have to control her future. On the other hand, there was a breakdown of communication somewhere—her dreams didn't get the memo!!!

Regina "Reggie" Reynolds

The bat comes down one more time to connect with my right knee. All I see is a streak of silver illuminated by a flash of lightning before it hits—no time to roll out of the way. An explosion of thunder rumbles with its unhindered force to surround the house, shaking the shingles loose to fly into the street. Its boom of destruction follows the lightning, dancing an electric explosion across the sky, amplifying the crunch of my knee as the bat shatters its existence. The sound is like that of gravel being displaced under hard-heeled boots and is followed by waves of agonizing pain rolling up my leg. I scream out of habit but know it won't help because the only one to hear it is the one causing the pain. He stands over me, eyes full of hatred and rage, still holding the bat in his right hand while reaching for his beer with the left. I try to gain balance on my hands and uninjured knee, but in doing so, I taste a thick, bloody mucus running from my nose into my mouth. I try to spit before it runs down my throat, feeding the sour nausea already churning in my stomach. I reach for the corner of the dining room table to pull myself up, but the pain is worse than the fear at this point, and I start to pass out.

The next blow is delivered with such force that it sends me flying from the floor into a set of glass shelves mounted on the wall, next to the door of the kitchen. The thick glass breaks into hundreds of large, jagged pieces pummeling downward, hitting a barrier of face and skull that slows their descent, but not the carnage they inflict along the way. The thick pieces of glass bounce with satisfaction as they hit the floor, leaving it discolored with crimson streaks of blood and pieces of my face. My last dance with the devil's darkness!

TABLE OF CONTENTS

Prologue iii
Chapter 1 1
Chapter 2 4
Chapter 3 14
Chapter 4 18
Chapter 5 29
Chapter 6 33
Chapter 7 41
Chapter 8 48
Chapter 9 53
Chapter 10 67
Chapter 11 75
Chapter 12 86
Chapter 13 92
Chapter 14 98
Chapter 15 106
Chapter 16 116
Chapter 17 122
Chapter 18 129
Chapter 19 136
Chapter 20 145
Chapter 21 152
Chapter 23 172

Chapter 24 179
Chapter 25 186
Chapter 26 187
Chapter 27 193
Chapter 28 200
Chapter 29 211
Chapter 30 221
Chapter 31 229
Chapter 32 232
Chapter 33 238
Chapter 34 242
Chapter 35 249
Chapter 36 255
Chapter 37 262
Chapter 38 271
Epilogue 276
THE END 281

Chapter 1

I want to breathe, fill my lungs with air, but I can't move. There's a heavy weight on my chest holding me still. But gradually, my breathing starts to slow, and I can feel my body begin to quiver and relax. I begin a sorrowful muttering as sleep begins to fade, and my eyes flutter open with the memory of pain and the ever-consuming fear. I feel the hot breath of *Suzie,* my seventy-pound, four-legged protector sprawled across my chest. She's a King German Shepherd who is just as damaged as I am, both mentally and physically. We take care of each other; we're a team.

I investigate her soulful, sad eyes as she begins to lick the salty tears from my face and whimper her understanding. The dreams are normal for Suzie and me, the supply of tears endless. She protects me as I dream, reliving my past, which plays over and over like reruns of a horror film where I'm the leading lady. The dreams depict what was once my life and are portrayed within the dreadful, endless tunnel of sleep. They're never the same, as I have many scenes and re-takes of violence and pain to pick from. Their sadistic humor lurks in the recesses of my mind, just waiting for sleep to come so the torment can begin. Suzie throws a *canine body block* across my chest at any sign of distress as I sleep. She witnessed one of my violent nightmares which threw me out of bed, using its darkness to propel me into the nightstand, causing more damage to my face. But what's another scar!

"It's okay, Suz, I'm fine," I mutter with a sick sadness in my voice. I wrap my arms around her and bury my wet face in her fur and squeeze tightly, whispering a sad, dependent thank you. When she has licked all the tears from my face, she turns her head and grabs her baby to deposit in my arms. She is comforted by the stuffed bunny and knows I will be too. She is a nurturer at heart, and I melt at the gesture. I wonder for the hundredth time how she can move forward. I know her past sorrows are just like mine, but she pushes them aside and thinks only of me. I lay there holding her and the stuffed animal, wishing I knew her secret.

I remember the day I found her and feel blessed every day. I had found myself sitting outside a King County Animal Shelter on one of Seattle's heavy rainy days. I was just released from the hospital after another long recovery, from yet another surgery, and vowed it would be my last.

Visibility through the windshield of my piece-of-crap Ford Explorer was like looking through thick Karo syrup as it ran down the glass in slow motion. The wipers didn't stand a chance of keeping up, so I reached out and turned them off, then dropped my hand back into my lap. The doctor, I had come to think of as a friend, told me I shouldn't be alone. He hoped I could move on and start dealing with my past. With concern showing in the furrow of his brow and gentle eyes, he reminded me I didn't have to be afraid any longer. But he'd seen with his eyes and held in his hands the parts of my body disfigured by torture and knew he was wasting his breath. Even as his words rushed out to comfort me, he knew I would always live with one foot in the dark, murky sludge that makes me who I am now. I don't think this is what he had in mind when he said I shouldn't be alone, but baby steps, right? So, before I could change my mind, I made sure my sweatshirt pocket held my driver's license and cash, then opened the car door, reminding myself of his words: *"You no longer have to be afraid."* What he didn't realize is the source of my fear may be gone—seriously gone, dead and buried gone—but the remembrance of horror the man left behind will always shadow my life.

Chapter 2

I entered the shelter through heavy double doors and saw the sign pointing to the reception area. The carpet was worn and dingy, showing visible signs that many visitors had walked this path looking for companionship and a friend. The smell of Pine Sol was strong and hit me like a heavy breeze, causing me to cough and my eyes to water instantly. I wiped my eyes dry as I approached the counter at the end of the hall, noticing the area was small, with just enough room for the staff to move around behind it. I took note of the two old computer terminals on each end, with stacks of paper and files in the middle. The literature plastered on every spare inch of the wall behind the counter was what you would expect. There were pictures of dogs and cats with their new owners, surrounded by many advertisements for different kinds of pet food and supplies. They looked like they had been there a while, as some of the corners had curled up and turned dingy. There was a chalkboard attached to the front of the counter that displayed, in bold, multicolored letters, a short list of information involved with adopting a pet.

All Costs For Neutering Services Are Included In Adoption Fee
All Adoptions Are Final
Dog Licenses Sold Here

I walked up to the counter and was greeted with what had become the "usual" stare. My face had healed as much as it was going to after three unsuccessful attempts to correct the damage. So, after the last try, I told my surgical team *enough* and refused any more hopeful procedures. You could call me pessimistic, but I was in control for once and was so done. I was getting used to the awkward glances and eyes full of pity that looked at me and then quickly looked away. I have a scar running from the middle of my forehead through my right eyebrow and splitting my eyelid down the middle. It continues to travel from there down through my cheek, stopping just below my jaw. The nerve damage to the right side of my face causes the corner of my mouth to present a permanent frown. The nerves in my eyelid were severed, leaving my eye curtained by dormant skin and the few lashes that remain.

The girl behind the counter was embarrassed by her behavior, trying instantly to replace her original reaction with a genuine smile. Her attempt failed miserably, however, and her eyes screamed how sorry she was. And there's that "pity" again. Her name tag said Rachel, and she looked to be in her early twenties. Her beauty was hidden by damaged orange and blue hair hanging limply to her shoulders, reminding me of colorful straw. Her eyes had been coated with heavy black eyeliner and thick, clumpy mascara, causing a raccoon effect. A large hoop nose ring displaying a tiny red rose dangled down to her mouth, finishing the persona. I just wanted to reach over the counter and scream, "WHY WOULD YOU DO THAT TO YOURSELF???" But at the same time, I envied her the freedom to make the choice. Hopefully, down the road in a few years, she'll see the same beauty I had. She'll wash away the hair color, heavy eyeliner, and remove the nose ring. Like magic, she'll be beautiful, and no surgery needed. BUT THEN AGAIN, I MAY BE BITTER! CORRECTION... I'M DEFINITELY BITTER!!!

"Hey there," Rachel said as she cleared her throat and pushed a few strands of limp blue straw behind her ear, not making eye contact. "What can I help you with today?"

"I would like to see the dogs you have for adoption," I said as my attention was drawn to the right of the counter where a gray metal door was pushed open by an employee, letting loose a barrage of barking before the door swung shut.

"Well, as you've just heard," she giggled while looking up, "we have a few ready and waiting." Her smile was genuine this time, pointing toward the door that had just swung shut, cutting off the sound of canines screaming, "Hey lady, I'm the one you want, pick me. I shouldn't be here; I didn't pee on the couch!!!"

She asked me to follow her and headed toward the same metal door where I assumed the kennels were located. We entered and were instantly greeted with the same onslaught of barking bouncing off the cement walls, following us as we made our way to the first kennel that housed an available adoptee. It was nonstop barking and out-of-control mayhem as dogs jumped on the chain-link fence of their kennels, running back and forth barking, "It's a mistake, I was framed, I shouldn't be here. Please pick me!!!" Every kennel was occupied with at least one dog and, in some cases, as many as four, depending on the breed and their temperament.

This was the quick education I received from Rachel as she made her way to the kennels that had dogs ready for new homes. Some of the kennel doors had names written on an erasable board with a black marker, and some didn't. I was told sometimes when families voluntarily give up their pets, they supply that information, along with a history of the pet and why they are bringing it to the shelter.

"Do you have kids?" Rachel asked as we continued walking. "I only ask because some of our dogs aren't good with little humans."

I cleared my throat and said bitterly, "No, I never had the chance." She gave me a sideways glance and nodded her head like she understood but didn't say anything. *If she only knew...*

There were only three cages that had dogs in them ready for adoption that day. I walked right past the first two without a glance inside; don't ask me why, I just had a feeling and headed directly to the last one. "What's the story on this one?" I couldn't take my eyes off the beautiful animal in the corner of the cage, and it saddened me to realize, just by looking at her, I already knew the story. Rachel reached over and pulled a clipboard off the top of a small table sitting to the left of the kennel.

She read through the information quickly before she spoke.

"She was left in the after-hours drop-off area late last week with no information supplied. She looks and behaves like she's had a tough time of it though, the poor thing. No one here has been able to bond with her. We do know that she's healthy for the most part, and her teeth show her to be about two years old. There are classic signs of abuse, however: shyness, nervousness, and of course, the visible scars. X-rays show her left front leg had a hairline fracture at one time but wasn't attended to, so it healed on its own, causing a slight limp. She doesn't seem to trust easily."

My first thought was, *I've found my soul mate.* "Any name listed?"

"Nope, not that I see here," Rachel said as she pointed to the clipboard.

I took a quick glance at Rachel and then slowly kneeled, as best I could, in front of the cage, hoping the slow movement would put the animal at ease. The poor thing was shaking and trying to push her entire body even further into the corner, turning her head into the cold cement wall. I started to talk softly through the chain-link fencing of the cage, hoping my voice would soothe her. I told her I wouldn't hurt her or yell, but she only blinked her mistrust, staring into the cold corner. I pulled myself up by holding onto the cage door and asked if I could go in.

"Sure," Rachel said, "take your time and I'll come back and check on you in a few."

I opened the door slowly, the sound of steel hinges sending out a loud intruding scream. I was sorry for the irritating shriek and apologized for it. I really didn't want to scare her, but unfortunately, the same grating screech rang out when I closed the door behind me. I waited for a bit, standing just inside the cage, speaking softly as a mother would to a sleeping child. At least, that's what I think a mother would do. Her deep brown eyes blinked as they gave me a quick glance before turning back to the corner. Her posture was rigid, front legs shaking, and her right ear was standing at attention and slightly twitching. I noticed her left ear had been ripped off jaggedly, leaving only a small piece of fur surrounded by bare skin that extended to the middle of her head. I asked her how she got hurt but only received the same nose twitch and blink. "Sorry, didn't mean to pry," I said. "Looks like you and I could swap some horror stories." She glanced my way again, but then right back to the wall. I looked around the cage and noticed her food dish was still full. "I'm guessing the food is pretty awful in here; you're not eating!" I got nothing this time. I moved slowly into the opposite corner and slid down to the floor, extending my right leg out in front of me. "Hope you don't mind if I sit a bit, I'm really tired. I got out of the hospital today and decided to come here and visit you." No response to that either. I sat in silence with her for a while on the cold cement. After a bit, her breathing started to slow, and her chest began moving rhythmically. She turned her head and looked directly at me, and I saw the sorrow in her beautiful eyes. "I understand, girl, I really do," I whispered.

She had the most beautiful coat I had ever seen on a dog, so thick and fluffy. A blending of black and gray shades donned her back and muzzle, her tail the same, but with soft white highlights. Her front and hind legs wore a salt-and-pepper mixture that traveled all the way down to her paws that were damaged by a couple of missing toes. The one ear she had left twitched under the harsh fluorescent light and sported the same blending of shades as her back. Her chest, broad and muscular, rippled with a combination of all hues. Her eyes were dark, beautiful spheres of color hiding unfathomable pain within their darkness. I touched my face and ran my finger along the scar on my cheek, letting her know we had a lot in common.

"Well, how are you two getting along?" Rachel asked, approaching the kennel.

Without even knowing it, I had made a decision. "I think we're going to get along just fine," I said, and pulled myself up to stand. "Let's get the paperwork out of the way now, and I'll be back first thing in the morning to sit a bit more with her before I take her home. I hope that's alright?"

"Absolutely," Rachel said with a huge smile, "any thoughts on a name?"

"I think I'll call her Suzie, spelled S-U-Z-I-E."

"Okay then, I'll see you at the desk."

"Well, goodbye Suzie, I'll see you tomorrow." I let myself out of the cage with the same grating sound I went in with, then slowly turned and latched the cage door, looking at her. "I told you I understand you; it's obvious we share scars. No one will ever hurt you again, I promise." I turned to leave and wiped a tear from my good eye as it slid down my cheek. With heavy feet, I moved slowly past the other kennels. With my eyes focused straight ahead, I didn't hear the mayhem as I passed the other cages. I couldn't get out of there fast enough. The sadness I know Suzie carried was chasing me to blend with mine. Determined to keep my promise to her, I pushed through the door and out to the reception area.

Chapter 3

I returned the next morning after a quick stop at the closest PetSmart to gather supplies. I decided on a neon pink collar and matching leash. I used one of those machines to create a name tag, which kept giving me a hard time with the spelling of Suzie's name. It kept correcting it to "Susie." Damn autocorrect is everywhere. Finally, I figured out how to use the manual option to spell the name the way I wanted it, and then listed my cell number. I had done some research on dog food the night before and decided the food with the most protein was the best. I got medium-sized stainless-steel bowls, some treats, a backpack, and the best item of all—a furry pink bunny. I walked into the shelter and up to the counter to find Rachel waiting for me. This time her smile was genuine, lighting up her face and touching her raccoon eyes.

"Good morning, it looks like you've been doing some shopping. Wow, that's some bright pink," Rachel says while pointing at the collar and leash. "I have all the adoption paperwork you signed yesterday in this envelope, and her rabies tag right here. If you hand me the collar, I'll put the tag on for ya." When she was done, she handed the collar back to me along with the paperwork, and then we headed to the kennel area to get Suzie. When we got to the cage, she was in the same spot as yesterday, still shaking uncontrollably and so nervous. But when she heard my voice, she turned her head and looked at me, then laid down with her head on her front paws. She never took her eyes off me as I entered the cage through the grating onslaught of noise. I was holding the bunny in my hand but had left the collar and leash sitting on the table outside.

"Rachel, I'm going to sit with her for a while before we go. I don't think she's ready yet."

"Sounds good, it looks like she calmed down some when she saw you though."

"Good morning, Suzie, I thought I would come back and sit for a bit, see if maybe you'd like to come home with me. Look, I brought you something," I say and wiggle the pink bunny in front of me. "It's a baby for you, I hope you like it." She lifted her head and blinked at the stuffed bunny, then watched me intently as I moved to the center of the cage and set it down. She continued to look at me while returning her head to her paws, never losing eye contact. I backed up slowly and decided to sit, bringing myself down to the same level. I hoped that would put her more at ease. I leaned back against the cold cement wall, bringing my good knee up to my chest to rest my chin. We continued looking at each other, using our eyes to tell one horrific story after another. With each blink of an eye, we shared individual acts of cruelty and a continual history of fear. There would be no secrets between Suzie and me.

Before long, a flash of multicolored fur rushed my way, a jolt of acceptance unfolding in mid-pounce. She moved quickly to the bunny, snatching it up with a soft mouth touch, bringing it to me. Her mouth was so close I could see her breath escaping around the bunny. Dark, loving eyes, only inches from mine, delivered a piercing message, *"I'm going to trust you, the damage is done; now we try to heal."* She stood there, not six inches away, trying to place the bunny in my hands. I took it and slowly reached up, tentative at first, to scratch behind her ear. She leaned into my hand, craving the warm, gentle touch. I buried my hand deeper into her soft fur, drawn to its warmth. She nuzzled the bunny in my hand and touched her forehead to mine. The warm closeness was a comfort and an act of trust for both of us. And before I knew it, she began licking my face clean of happy tears. I didn't realize I had started to cry, craving the same gentleness and affection she did. We were a sight to see when Rachel came back to the cage, me crying and Suzie devouring my tears like they were an addictive drug. That was a good day, and the doctor was right, I didn't have to be alone anymore.

Chapter 4

My phone begins ringing from where it lays on the nightstand, pulling me back to the present with its rude intrusion. Suzie shifts to my side as I wipe my eyes quickly, throwing my hair off my face. I look at the clock illuminating the time, 11:17 p.m. The caller ID on my cell says it's Michael. I look over at Suzie telling her who it is. She's instantly alert and sits up, putting her paw on my knee. I reach up and give her a quick scratch under her chin, "Sorry, Suz, looks like we're going back to work."

"Hello," I say through the thick, heavy residue of an all too familiar nightmare.

"Hi, Reggie," he says with exhausted resignation, "I know it's late, but Mickey's needed again!"

With a resigned whisper, I ask, "How bad is it?"

I sit up and slide to the headboard, propping pillows behind me to have some comfort as I lean back. I place my hand protectively around Suzie and settle in for what I know is going to be another horrific story. It won't be a unique story, just another version of the same, like plagiarized chapters of some other victim's life. The main thing is; if Michael is calling for help, we have a chance to write a new ending.

"It's bad, Reggie, she's lucky to be alive."

That sounded familiar, that was me three years ago, and many others in-between. I was so tired of hearing that phrase, "lucky to be alive." But all I can do is let out a painful sigh and say, "Let's hear it."

"She was brought into the ER about 7:30 this evening by her husband who claims it was an accident. He said he was doing some gardening in the backyard, digging holes to plant a hedge, and had a shovel in his hands. He says she 'snuck' up from behind and startled him; his reflexes kicked in, and he turned and hit her with the shovel accidentally. Can you believe that? Hit her with a shovel, saying it was an accident!!! Well, that shovel accidentally hit her more than once, there's so much damage. She's so scared, all she does is answer questions with a shake of her head, but only after looking at him before doing so. She has multiple gashes on both arms and legs from the shovel head. Her face took most of the rage from this 'accident,' it's nothing but swollen, multicolored meat. I can't believe she's still conscious! There's so much swelling to her right eye, both cheeks, and nose, he must have used the back of the shovel head to administer multiple blows. I can only hope there isn't any permanent damage to the eyesight in her right eye. Unfortunately, we have to wait for the swelling to go down in her face before we can assess all the damage. I'm going in now to repair a nasty gash to her forehead where her hairline was ripped back about three inches. And then I'll take a look at all the gashes to her arms and hands to see what needs stitching there. She was trying to protect her face but failed horribly. At this point, the swelling to her face is so severe we won't be able to assess all the damage for days."

"Where's the husband now?"

"Oh, he's right by her side, won't leave her alone. He keeps squeezing her hand and telling her how stupid she was to sneak up on him like that. Didn't she know that was dangerous? The son-of-a-bitch hasn't once said he was sorry and won't make eye contact with any of my staff or myself."

"Please tell me no kids!" I look at Suzie, praying; *please no, please no.*

"No. No kids thank God."

I let out a thankful breath before moving on. "What's the history? Has Abby been able to find anything?"

"Yes, that's why I'm calling you so late. Our patient, Clarissa Troy, has been seen in almost all of the ER departments in the city; apparently, she's very 'accident' prone!!!"

"I know this is a stupid question, but has she ever filed charges?" I knew the answer before Michael could respond; women in this situation know better than to talk to the police. It just makes things worse for them. Besides, a restraining order is just a piece of paper, and paper is a useless form of protection. But most importantly, there's the threat of harm to their children and loved ones, so they stay silent. That's how an abuser wields his sadistic control.

I'm not saying society turns a blind eye to domestic violence—not at all. There are county and city facilities out there who do what they can. They try to help, but the reality of being understaffed and underfunded makes these facilities temporary, and then where do the victims go??? Right back to their abuser.

"Abby couldn't find anything, and believe me, she was thorough. That woman is a methodical, protective mama when she's working on a case."

"Don't I know it," I say with an agreeable sigh. Instinctively, I bring my right knee up to run my hand over it and my leg protectively. I'm still in awe of their artificial perfection, as the last chapter of my horror flashes through my mind. I mentally turn the pages and begin to relive the explosion of memories leaping off the last page. I remember the piercing pain and hard work of rehab. I remember the orthopedic surgeon explaining how damaged my leg was. I see him pointing to the X-ray with a steady hand, showing me what was coming. He would replace my knee but needed to replace my femur with a titanium rod first... "Close the freakin' book, Reggie!" I scream inside.

"How long do you figure you can keep her in the hospital without the husband getting suspicious?"

"It's hard to say, a week to ten days, if we're lucky. She needs a lot of pain medication just to function at this point. And like I said, until the swelling goes down around her eye, we won't know if there's permanent damage to her sight. So, the longer we can keep her here the better, both for her recovery and her own safety at this point."

"Do we have eyes?"

"I called John the minute I examined her and heard the story. He put a team on alert waiting for instructions. He's here at the hospital and won't let the husband out of his sight."

I run my hands over my eyes and respond, resigned to the fact that we're heading into another storm of human atrocity and betrayal. "That's good," I say. John and I have worked together on every case since the beginning; he's the best. He's ex-military and good at hiding in plain sight, where I am not. My mind begins to race as it takes the lead, bombarding me with possible plans of attack. Over and over, the idea bubbles start popping up above my head, dancing with different ideas. But the truth is I won't be able to form a plan until I speak with Clarissa and learn as much as I can about her husband.

Suzie moves closer and sniffs my neck with her cold nose before resting her head on my shoulder. "It's okay, Suz, we'll help her," I whisper as Michael takes a deep breath on the other end of the phone. I can hear his breathing slow, even over the phone as he wills himself to calm down. Sometimes I think I even hear his blood pressure rise to its limit when he describes the atrocities men inflict on women they profess to love. He's a good man and an excellent doctor, who has never allowed the horrific realities he sees to pull him down to wallow in that darkness. Thank goodness after all the carnage he's seen, he hasn't become jaded and given up. He's not one of those people who pass judgment when they haven't walked in the shoes of a victim of domestic violence. The ones who can't come close to understanding the dynamics of the situation, so they throw up their hands and state, "The woman has a choice; she can leave!" But the truth is vulgar and unfathomable. It's a horrible beast continually changing its face to devour each individual victim's identity. No person should judge or imply that it is that black and white. The blending of the gray shadows of viciousness is delivered on many different levels and degrees of unthinkable violence. I would give anything to be one of the individuals who are so naive they actually believe it's that easy to get out, where they are comfortable with living with their head in the sand. Those are the clueless lucky ones, and I pray that someday there will be way more naiveté to this brutality than victims. But it's not a medical condition like cancer or diabetes, where we can hold a telethon to raise money for research and make strides toward a cure. No, the devil has too many minions on his payroll, and he has trained them well.

"How's our Suzie?" he asks because he hears me reassure her that we will help.

I smile before responding, as Michael loves her as much as I do. He's tried for the longest time to figure out how she knows what she knows and does what she does. She's a canine enigma, and he will always be extremely grateful to her for standing guard and protecting me from my past horror. She's my protective sentry, always trying to level out the damage that comes along with being pulled back into the brutal reality of darkness. "She's her usual motherly self," I say, giving her a squeeze. "Okay, send the file to my email and have Abby get a packet ready just in case. I'll be in touch after I take a look."

"I already sent the medical info that I have to Abby by messenger so she can combine it with her search results. She'll scan it and send it to your email and have a packet delivered by one of the runners. What luxurious location are you staying at this time?" he asks with noticeable sarcasm.

"Motel 6 off Winston, room 122."

"OH MY GOD! Reggie, that's almost the ghetto!"

"Actually, it *is* the ghetto," I say to myself. I hang up before he can rant any further; we've been through this before. It's better if I move around, travel light, and never stay in one place for more than about ten days. I always stay in motels that can offer me two adjoining rooms on the ground floor, preferably in the back. I deal only in cash, drive my inconspicuous old Ford, and do my best to stay hidden if I can. Let's face it, no pun intended, but my face *is* unforgettable. These precautions we take are not only beneficial to helping the Rescued, but for the safety of Suzie and myself. If we stay safe, the Rescued are safe, and hopefully, their healing can begin. Not just the healing of physical injuries, but most importantly, the emotional ones. Hopefully, they can find the strength to travel the road to trusting again. It's the longest road anyone can travel; I know because I'm still stumbling down that road, crossing the yellow line at times. I'm able to take small detours these days but eventually end up back on the main highway, counting the reflectors down the middle, waiting for the "TRUST" exit to appear. Like I said, it's a long road that has many stops and starts.

All victims in a dire situation of domestic violence can only believe in one kind of trust, the kind that shows them pain and darkness. They trust only in the knowledge of reading his mood as he comes through the door at night. The trust in seeing the signs of anger as they grow. The trust of knowing when the first blow will be delivered no matter how much she tries to please. The trust in recognizing the pain will come even if she does everything to his liking. The trust that once one chore is mastered, he will add another and another to the circle of abuse. The circle will never end; that's the trust she knows.

So, it's a long road for all of us, but the miles can be traveled with time and patience. The goal is to help the Rescued begin to realize the trust we offer is far from the trust they've known. When they start believing there's a difference, they can begin to trust in themselves and start to realize there is hope. They can become stronger and slowly find the pieces of themselves they were forced to lose. They just have to believe, believe that this is a new beginning, and they deserve it. That's never easy because by the time we step in, they haven't been allowed to think or make decisions on their own for years. That's another one of our difficult hurdles. No woman is the same; no situation mirrors another except for one factor, *FEAR*. It's a dark monster that controls and manipulates, sending its cancer out to consume all the light and hope of its chosen victim. It coils its evil around every shred of self-respect and dignity, stomping on its strength and not stopping until it has beaten down all trust and self-worth. Each victim was once a loving, vital woman, who was turned into an empty shell that now believes she deserves this life. The heavy cloak of fear wraps itself so tight it restricts the heart from beating while immobilizing the whole body.

Chapter 5

I lean over and kiss Suzie on her forehead murmuring, "I need a shower." I slide out of bed and head for the bathroom. Stopping at the window, I pull apart the curtains to glance out at the darkness. It's going to be a long night. I flip on the bathroom light and look in the mirror. My T-shirt is covered in nightmare sweat and clinging tightly to my chest, along with the dog hair that decided to join the party. "Great," I mutter to myself as I start rummaging through the clothes decorating the tile at my feet. Hopefully, I can find something that doesn't smell too bad and hasn't been slept in.

My shower is quick and to the point. No shaving of legs or armpits, and no sweet smells wafting off my wet skin from a silky body wash. I quickly dry off and put my yoga pants back on with the most presentable white tank top I can find. Pulling my hair back into a wet ponytail, I dry my face completely and begin the only ritual I have, besides brushing my teeth, of course. I break open a Vitamin E capsule and apply the soothing liquid to the scars on my face. Maybe someday it will make a difference.

I empty Suzie's water dish and refill it before I grab the dog food bag and measure out the cup and a half of food I allow her morning and night. She gives me the usual stink eye, its translation being: *"Are you sure you measured right?"* I playfully tug her good ear, look into those beautiful questioning eyes, and reassure her I did. I grab my laptop off the nightstand, rearrange the pillows at the headboard of the bed before settling in, and then log into my email. Just as promised, Abby's attachment is there, waiting for me to take Clarissa's dark journey. It's time to try and get comfortable with the uncomfortable, for Clarissa's sake.

I skim over the medical terms which I have personally heard and seen too many times. I even know their meanings, saving me time as I search out the personal data. According to her driver's license, Clarissa Troy is thirty-one years old, weighs 115 pounds, and stands 5'3" tall with blue eyes and dark blonde hair. She lives at 3303 West Mission Blvd, in Seattle, Washington. The date of her first ER visit was March 20, 2007, where she told the nurse she was running up her front steps and tripped, hitting her face on the railing of the porch. She was sent home after receiving five stitches below her left eye. Over the last nine years, she has been seen in various emergency rooms around the Tacoma and Seattle area, twelve times that we know of. But for every injury she had treated in the ER, I know from personal experience there are just as many, or more that weren't. Incidents where she endured injuries she felt weren't bad enough to be put through the shame of another hospital visit and the new lie as to how it happened. *"If only the walls of 3303 West Mission Blvd could talk."*

From this information, I am able to put together what I call an "escalation pattern." Each documented visit more creative in its explanation of what caused her injuries, each new X-ray screaming "not possible," while portraying the undeniable damage. Each time she was treated, she was asked if she wanted to speak with someone privately, and each offer was refused. She was asked if she felt safe in her home, she stated yes. This is not unusual; in fact, it's the norm in abuse cases. I shiver with deep-seated anger and shame when I'm reminded of how many times I gave the same answers, played the same fabricated game.

I set my laptop aside and slide off the bed. I need a glass of wine before I can continue reading the reports and calling Michael to discuss my thoughts. I'm thinking a very big glass as I head for the small refrigerator in the corner of my room.

"Hi," I say after Michael picks up, "I've just finished going over the information. You're right about being lucky; I don't think she has much time left if she goes home with him. I'm going to need your help to see her without her husband knowing; any ideas?"

Chapter 6

It's 9:00 o'clock the next morning, and Suzie and I are on our way to the hospital. After two glasses of wine and a long phone conversation with Michael ending early this morning, we decided I should come to the hospital to meet with Clarissa. This way, Michael can manipulate an excuse to separate her from her husband, so we can meet in private. I glance at Suzie in the back seat and follow her painful dance back and forth, from window to window. She's anticipating what's to come, knows what we will go through, and hopes we both have the strength to do this again. Her baby is carried gingerly in her mouth, her whines of motherly assurance filling the back seat as I make my way down the highway. I don't know if the assurances are for me, her baby, or herself. All I know is she won't be able to settle down until this is over.

"It's okay, Suz, we'll help her if she lets us," I say, trying to calm her. She's heard it all before but keeps up her vigil. I look in the mirror to make eye contact, and sensing this, she stops pacing for just a second to lock onto my concern. In her eyes, I see years of exhaustion and sadness unlike any other, a cloudy film of suffering hides within those beautiful spheres. She carries each story in her heart wrapped in its own sadness. She's not able to look at the happy endings, as there was too much pain to get there. I think about all the women we've helped, all the lives we've had a part in changing. I remember each woman vividly, each individual story, each sorrowful chapter of why our paths crossed. They will forever be my distant sisters, filling a void in my heart. I don't know where they ended up, what their names are now, or what they decided to do with their lives. Once they're safe, I never have contact with them again; it's for the best, that's how this works. At least for me.

Seattle's traffic is always heavy, and this morning is no different. At this rate, it will take me at least an hour to get to the hospital. But over the years, I've become used to the dynamics of the big city, and the traffic doesn't bother me anymore. Suzie, however, has never been very patient, especially when she knows someone needs our help. I put in a Blues CD, keeping the volume low the way Suzie likes it. A soothing saxophone medley wafts from the speakers, working its magic; she slows her pacing and then stops. With her baby still cradled in her mouth, she lays down, placing her head on her paws. As my Explorer inches forward a few feet at a time, my mind starts to wander to the past. Back to the day Michael and Abby invited me to their beautiful home, presenting me with an idea that changed our lives forever.

I remember feeling so out of place driving up the hillside in the city of Madrona, I just knew I was going to get pulled over and questioned. And Suzie, being Suzie, wasn't helping any by sticking her large head out the back window with strings of moist slobber flapping in the wind. She'd shake her head violently, unlocking the wet streams to fly off and attach themselves to the back window. The streams tried valiantly to stick in place, clinging like skinny transparent slugs screaming, *"Mayday, Mayday,"* while slithering along the glass. "Classy, Suz, if we get stopped let me do the talking," I say as I glance to the right and see Lake Washington displayed in full color. It was early July, and the sun was making its not-so-often appearance to encompass the unbelievable scene below. "Only the rich have this view!!!" I continue on until I find the address

Michael had given me, letting out a low whistle as I travel through the open security gate. "We're not in Kansas anymore, Suz," I whisper as I follow the circle drive around to stop at the foot of welcoming stone steps. "Best behavior for both of us, girlfriend," I said as I opened my door, stepping out and adjusting my sunglasses.

Michael stepped out of the large double doors at the top of the steps and waved. The doors were made of stained glass and caught the sunlight as they swung out, throwing quick prisms of color my way as they did so. He was wearing jeans, a button-down cotton striped shirt, and running shoes. He placed his sunglasses on as he moved down the steps to greet me. I tried to remember if I had ever seen him in anything but his white coat and tie; the change was nice, he looked relaxed. As I walked toward him, Suzie stuck her head out the window and whimpered. We both turned, and with canine irritation, she tilted her head to one side, informing us she couldn't open the door herself. Laughing, Michael turns to me and says, "Abby wants to meet both of you."

We entered the house, and I was instantly hit with a sense of home. This massive place screamed

"WELCOME" and made you immediately feel at ease. It wasn't flashy or overdone; it was comfortable and inviting. "Michael, this place is amazing," I say as we move through the foyer into a beautiful office off to the right. The room was done in soft colors, overstuffed inviting furniture, and plush rugs lying atop a dark bamboo floor. Its warmth reached out, encouraging you to kick off your shoes, flounce down on one of the soft couches indicating you should grab the TV remote on the way. At the far end of the room and up three steps, situated directly in the center, was a large glass top desk. The only items on it were a computer, printer, and a vase of deep-colored, red roses. The outside wall behind the desk was made of glass, with French doors that opened to an amazing deck where you could stand and devour the picturesque view of Lake Washington below. But the view you saw when entering the room was only blue sky and clouds, making you feel like you were floating, and with one big jump off the deck, you could bounce onto a cloud and be enveloped in its softness.

I heard a slight click to my left and turned just in time to see a woman enter with a younger version of Michael following. "There you are," Michael said as he moved past me to put his arm around the woman and give a nod to the younger man. "Reggie, this is my wife, Abby, and our son, John." I look from one to the other and am instantly drawn in; the son has his father's eyes and solid stature. He was wearing a solid black T-shirt, cargo pants, and black lace-up heavy boots. "John has done three tours overseas and has recently returned and opened his own security firm," Michael informs me, before reaching over and giving his son's shoulder a squeeze. John stepped forward slowly and extended his hand my way, making direct eye contact as he did so. I didn't see pity in his eyes when he saw my face; just a hard understanding crossed his features and then a comforting smile. I reached out and took his hand tentatively, keeping a comfortable distance between us. At that time, closeness was still a very raw issue for me, but I was working on it.

"Thank you for your service, John," I said before dropping my eyes to the floor, losing contact.

"Of course," he said and stepped back next to his parents.

"Reggie, this is my wife, Abby," Michael says as he turns to the woman next to him and smiles.

Abby was the most unpretentious, regal woman I had ever seen. The combination of those characteristics was hard to fathom, as they were so different from each other. She had warm eyes that drank you in and a demeanor to match. I kept wondering how someone could be wearing jeans and a sweater and look like she should be attending a gala at the same time. Her coal-black hair was pulled back from her face and held at the nape of her neck with a silver clip. She wore only a touch of makeup and only small, diamond stud earrings. She extended her arms and moved to embrace me but noticed my slight retreat as she did so. Within a split second, she understood her mistake, changing the beginning of an embrace to a soft handshake instead. "Forgive me," she whispered and squeezed my hand. "Please, let's all sit and get to know each other." We moved to the sitting area and all sat down on the plush furniture in an awkward silence. Suzie sat to my right and was extremely pleased with the fact she was allowed to be included. "So, you must be Suzie," Abby said with a smile that actually touched her eyes with its sincerity. Suzie turned her head my way and blinked.

"It's okay," I say and motion for her to go. Suzie stands and moves past Michael with a quick look and stops at Abby's feet. Abby reached out to touch the soft fur around Suzie's neck as her face lit up like a child on Christmas morning.

"You're beautiful, Suzie, and very special I'm told." After lapping up the praise and affection, Suzie looked back at me and then turned her head to John. Once again, I said it was okay. She stood and moved around the coffee table to then deposit her beautiful self at John's feet. They stared at each other for what seemed like minutes, each one sizing the other up, wondering if they liked each other.

"Hey, gorgeous, you busy Saturday night?" Suzie barked and placed her paw on John's knee, giving him her biggest smile. "Looks like Suzie's a flirt," John said, laughing.

"She's not the only one," Michael said and shook his head. But after that display of flirting, all the awkwardness had left the room, and I was able to relax a bit. I have always trusted Suzie's instincts to protect me, letting her take the lead where humans were concerned. Her body language, and the flirty smile she just flashed John, told me these are good people.

Chapter 7

Abby cleared her throat and began. "We asked you to come by today to first, listen to a personal story and then listen to an idea stemming from that story." I looked at the three of them, locking eyes with each one individually, then sat back, nodding my head. Suzie moved back to my side to sit sentry, leaning into my hand that automatically touched her head and stroked, bringing both of us comfort. Her only concern at this point was me and how the story we were about to hear would emotionally run me over and send me back to my past. Looking back now, I know she sensed sadness in these people and wanted to comfort me as I listened.

Michael reached out and took Abby's hand lovingly, encouraging her to continue. "It's okay, baby," he said. All it took was his touch, and she seemed to sit up straighter and become stronger. What I would have given for a fraction of that closeness and love. She nodded her head and turned my way.

Abby began, "Two years ago, we lost my sister to domestic violence; she was brutally murdered by her husband," she stated with visible numbness. "He was just sentenced to life without parole and we"—she motioned with her hand to Michael and John—"are now ready to move on. Michelle was two years older than I, and we were very close growing up and into adulthood. She was my Maid of Honor when Michael and I got married, and she is, was, John's Godmother. They were extremely close also," she said, lifting her head to look at her son. "About four years ago, she met Marcus, her husband, at a fundraiser we were chairing. Michelle and I both sat on many boards and managed to raise a lot of money for medical research." She glanced at her husband and said, "That's how Michael and I met. Anyway, I had never seen her so happy; she fell head over heels for him. We all liked him at first, but the more I think about it, that was because she was so happy, we never saw past that to get to really know him. If we had, maybe she'd still be with us."

As Abby delivered her story, I witnessed the change in this strong woman. An overwhelming regret and sadness showed within the gradual slump of her shoulders, and guilt was worn on her face like heavy foundation. Her hands betrayed her strength as they shook while wiping away the devastation of loss that was leaking from her eyes. Once composed, she was able to continue. "After they married, he moved her across the country to Baltimore where he took a position with Johns Hopkins. He was a leading neurosurgeon and was elected to sit on the board there. After about six months, I noticed the phone calls were fewer, which was strange because we were always so close and talked every day. We lost our parents as young adults and were thrown into the business of handling the 'family money.' Every time I reached out, she never picked up. I must have left hundreds of messages for her. When she did return my calls, it was always at strange times and always from a payphone or an unknown landline, never her home phone or cell. I started to notice she never laughed anymore when she called, and her voice was always soft and full of sadness, saying she couldn't talk long."

I sat very still, watching the three people in front of me, and tried to put myself in their shoes. Trying to relate to the overwhelming helplessness and worry they must have lived with constantly. This is an area I never had to worry about. I was raised in the system, so when my life and bad choices decided to kick me in the ass, there was no one out there to notice something was wrong. The sad truth is an abuser works long and tirelessly to take complete control of their victim by isolating them from all family and friends anyway. So eventually, they are just as alone as I was.

"Eventually, Michael and I decided we needed to go and see for ourselves what was going on. We arrived at their house early one evening and were greeted at the door by Marcus stinking of booze and hate in his eyes. In no uncertain terms, he told us to get off his porch and leave. I insisted on seeing Michelle, but he just smiled and said she wasn't in any shape to receive visitors. I couldn't believe what I was hearing, so I tried to push past him into the house, calling out for my sister. I saw her standing at the top of the stairs with two black eyes and a cut lip bleeding down the front of her nightgown. Michael tried to go to her, but Marcus stepped in the way and said he was calling the police. Michelle cried from the top of the stairs for us to leave and tried to assure us everything was going to be alright. She said it was all her fault they got into a fight, that Marcus didn't mean to hurt her, and he was sorry. Marcus, however, didn't seem sorry at all and just showed us the door."

As the blanket of sadness wrapped itself around this family, I was drawn in, trying to figure out why they were sharing such a personal story with me. They knew I had stood in Michelle's shoes, but if they were waiting for me to share my story, that wasn't going to happen. My story certainly wasn't unique, but it was mine. Besides, Michael knew the last chapter of it anyway.

Abby continued, "A few weeks after our visit to Baltimore, I received a call from a detective informing me Michelle had been killed by her husband, and would I be available to make the trip to identify her body. After the initial shock of hearing this, I pulled myself together and was able to ask how he knew it was Marcus. He informed me Marcus called 911 and said his wife was stabbed and dying. When the paramedics and police arrived, it was too late for Michelle, but Marcus was sitting beside her on the floor, covered in blood and still holding the knife. When asked what happened, he just said, 'She deserved it!' He never even tried to save himself after he was arrested."

The room became dreadfully quiet as I looked from one to the other. "I'm so sorry to hear that, and I'm glad you're ready to move on. But I'm a little confused as to why you brought me here to share this. Is there something I can do for you?"

Abby cleared her throat and tried to calm her nerves before speaking. "I mentioned my sister and I were left with the task of handling the family fortune, which is huge! Then when Michelle died, she listed John and me as beneficiaries of her estate, adding even more zeros to the balance sheet. I've been blessed with a knack for investing and can make money grow, so now it's just obscene. To be blunt, we have enough money to buy a number of small countries a dozen times over."

I sat there stunned, thinking this is so bizarre; maybe they want me to help them spend their money. "Hell yes! Sign me up!" I leaned forward, putting my elbows on my knees and took a deep breath. I still couldn't formulate a thought as to why they were telling me this. Finally, I spoke, "And… I'm sensing all those zeros are a problem for you?" It took about five seconds of silence before John burst out laughing, and it didn't take long for the rest of us to follow. "I don't mind saying I'm really confused right now!"

After the laughter died down, I looked at Abby as she blew her nose and wiped away her tears. "Well, no, not a problem exactly. We want something good to come from Michelle's death. We want to use all those zeros to help women in those situations break away and be safe, help them start over. That's why we reached out to you. You made it out, and we want you to educate us on how we can make this work."

I sat in silence, trying to decide if these three people had any idea what this would take and how many individuals needed to be willing to help, not to mention keep their mouths shut. I wondered if they could actually understand the danger each and every one of us would be in. Call it secrecy or anonymity, we would have to hide in the shadows and stay behind the scenes. But whatever we called it, no woman we chose to help would be safe unless we protected ourselves first. They were right about one thing; I did make it out, but not by my own hand. I didn't suddenly stand up and say enough is enough and fight back. No, it was either fate or karma that jumped in to save me that night, and I'm still asking myself why. I will always feel a need to do penance for not being strong enough to do it myself.

Chapter 8

Over the next few weeks, we huddled together over lunches and dinners to prioritize our plans moving forward. First came finding a location for us to work out of; once that was done, we could figure out the rest. We all added our own thoughts as to what the building floor plan should be in order to meet our many anticipated needs. Second, we had a shopping list put together by John's security team for the endless amounts of equipment needed. However, it didn't take us long to realize the list would grow and grow the further our planning stage progressed. Once that was in the works, we nailed down security procedures to make sure we weren't vulnerable from any direction, and that led to establishing protocols for as many scenarios as we could come up with. We knew we would learn as we went but felt we had a good start. We needed to protect ourselves from all walks of life.

Domestic violence touches the poor, middle class, and rich; it doesn't give a damn about race or age, or even gender; it simply doesn't discriminate.

It has worked diligently to worm its way into all walks of life; no entity is ignored, and no one is immune from its darkness. The creator of this violence sends out tentacles to slither and search; craving the hunt and is delighted when it finally finds the perfect host to immerse itself into. The host needs to be weak enough that the transformation is easy and final; the creator has his plans, and the host must deliver them. There are no guidelines for the host to follow when picking a victim; all that's required is it delivers the violence as the leader of this ancient cult instructs. In my mind, the leader has taken on many personas over the years, but he goes by the name "Devil" in our circles.

We needed to be diligent and not create an electronic or paper trail. Our computers and cell phones could be hacked if either one of us is careless, forgetting the importance of true diligence. If an abuser isn't tech-smart, he can hire someone who is. Depending on their profession, they can use everything at their disposal to track down any one of us. They can hack into our lives and find out where we live and what vehicle we drive. We needed to remember, if we can find a back way into acquiring the information we need, they can too. With all that taken into account, we finally were able to outline each of our responsibilities. We make a good team and through the process of putting this together, I realized that these three people had grown to mean a lot to me; I think of them as family, and that's major for me. That's when my first barrier started crumbling.

It was after one of our strategy sessions that I had the chance to ask Abby a question that had wormed itself into my brain. We were standing in the kitchen as she poured us each a glass of expensive Chardonnay. It was funny that the two of us being so different shared a passion for wine. Her passion, of course, was on a grander scale than mine as we were drinking from beautiful Baccarat Crystal goblets, not the plastic cups I unwrap in my motel room. She commented on the vintage and year of the label as she handed me my glass, "Oh, excuse me, goblet." I had no idea what she was talking about because I didn't hear, "Barefoot Chardonnay" for $7.99 a bottle at all. One thing I can say in defense of my obvious classlessness is my bottle of wine always has a cork—no twist tops or boxes for me.

"So," I said, "I was wondering if Michelle had a nickname while growing up."

Abby brought her beautiful eyes to mine but didn't speak for a few minutes. She was pondering the question that just came out of the blue, wondering where this was going. Finally, she spoke, "Why do you ask?"

"Well, we've been working so hard to build something to honor her, and we can't even call it by her name. Because of all the anonymity involved and security we have put in place, we can't take a chance of that being a weak link. However, I thought that if we used a nickname, her nickname, it could be our way of honoring Michelle while we make her legacy work. We could use the nickname when referring to us as a team." I waited for a response as I sipped my wine, watching the proposal play across Abby's face. I could see the memories of her sister in her eyes before they escaped down her cheek, riding within the wetness of a tear. She wiped it away slowly and offered me a sad smile, delivered with love. To this day, I still feel that smile was directed at me as unconditional gratitude and a number of other emotions I was beginning to be exposed to. She moved closer and tentatively reached out her hand to my face, it wavered there slightly, waiting for me to pull away. When I didn't, her warm hand touched my cheek, surprising us both with the contact. I had a breakthrough that day, in that kitchen, with that loving woman. I never thought that would happen to me.

"Mickey," she said with a smile, "Daddy always called her Mickey."

Chapter 9

As I pull into the parking lot of the hospital, I call Michael. He tells me to continue around back and park in front of the maintenance department entrance; John will be there to meet me. Sure enough, as I turn the corner, he's already holding the door open, waiting for me to pull in. I turn around and speak to Suzie, trying to reassure her. She will have to wait in the Ford, and I know it'll be a horrible vigil as always when we're separated. "I'll be fine, John is here," I say and point to the door. She licks my face and whines, telling me with her eyes to be careful and tries to give me her baby. "No, you take care of her," I whisper, trying to assure her I'll be back soon. Opening the car door, I begin to wipe away the nose snot Suzie left on my sunglasses before putting them back on. Then I turn and walk to the door where John is waiting, pulling up the hood of my sweatshirt along the way.

"How is she?" John asks while looking at Suzie through the driver's side window, where she has positioned herself to wait for me.

"Protective and motherly, like always," I say and slip through the door.

"I just sent Dad a text and told him we're on our way up. He told Clarissa's husband she needed more X-rays and it would take about an hour. That guy is going bat-shit crazy already, having her out of his sight." I reach up and pull my hood lower to hide my face as much as possible. John is wearing hospital scrubs, making him look like he belongs, but my appearance is a different story. We don't want anyone recognizing us or making a connection to Clarissa if this doesn't work out. Even though we have a lot of sympathetic hospital staff here who help us, we can never be too careful. If we aren't successful helping Clarissa, we'll end up doing this again for someone else and need to rely on their discretion to keep us safe. We go down a short hall and climb two flights of gray metal stairs. As we open the door on the second floor, we turn left, heading to the double doors marked X-ray. We don't go through them, however; instead, we stop in front of a windowless door to the right. John opens the door just enough to let me enter.

"Thanks," I say and step into a small room used for patients waiting their turn for X-rays. There's a soft light on the wall above the bed, casting an eerie glow to the room and the bandaged occupant huddling under warm blankets. The room is small, and the hospital bed takes up most of the space. There literally is no room for anything else but a hard-plastic chair in the corner, sitting cold and unoccupied.

"Let me know when you're ready," he says while standing back from the door. "We'll have eyes on the husband the entire time."

After the door closes behind me, I remove my hood and sunglasses. Clarissa Troy's face and head are covered completely with gauze, leaving only a line for her mouth and a hole for her right eye, which blinks at me in surprise, or could be horror. "My name is Reggie," I say while keeping as much eye contact as I can. She doesn't say a word, just stares. Slowly, I take out my cell phone and snap a picture of her, then move slowly around the bed and stand close. I show her the phone and watch her reaction. Even though her face is hidden by a curtain of white gauze, it screams shame. A single tear is trapped in the corner of her un-bandaged eye, soaking the surrounding sterile barrier protecting the rest of her face. "I was here before just like you are, all wrapped up in the protection of white gauze. Hoping it was a magic cloak, hoping it had the power to heal the wounds left by my husband." I let that hang in the air, and she begins to shake her head violently, instantly regretting the movement. With hands that look like they've been pushed through a cheese grater, she reaches up to hold her head tenderly. "Look at me, Clarissa!" Slowly she does as I ask, bewilderment and mistrust dancing in her eye as she focuses on me with defeat. I see, more than hear, a sigh as her shoulders slump. "As you can see, there was no magic for me under that gauze. I've seen this too many times, Clarissa. If you stay with him, you won't have to worry about living with disfigurement and shame, because you won't be alive to care." Her eye studies my face, traveling down the jagged scar of my past, realizing with clarity she could be looking into the mirror of her future. I see so much sorrow in that eye, I can relate to its story as it oozes pain. The IV drip of surrender and defeat hangs above her head, continuing to send cold reminders through her arm to flood her body. With self-loathing blanketing her entire being, she manages to look at the picture on my phone again. I continue to be aggressive, because I want more than anything to reach her, to make her understand. "I'm still alive, Clarissa, and I can help *you* stay alive too!" I say it hard and cold, wanting her to get the message because we don't have much time.

"NO, NO, NO," she mutters as she tries to shake her head again. "I've tried, and he won't let me go. You have to leave; he'll find a way to get back here and it will be worse." Translation: worse for her. The terror in her voice is consuming every inch of her as she pleads, "Please, just go, if he finds me with you, he'll come up with some new sadistic way to let me know he owns me, to punish me!" With each phrase, her voice and body language begin to skyrocket out of control. The panic inside escalates by the fact she knows he's out in the hospital somewhere totally seething because he isn't in control of her. Each minute that passes causes him to reach new heights of anger, knowing he will blame her for causing him distress. "Please just tell them to take the X-rays and leave me alone."

"Look, I know this is unexpected, but I was sent by a friend to help you, please let me!"

"Who are you?" Her question is delivered with bitterness and mistrust, mostly mistrust. "You don't know me!"

"I know everything about you, Clarissa," I say in a painful, all-knowing whisper. "I know all the lies you've told out of shame and personal humiliation. I've brushed away all your painful and hopeless tears. I've felt every single stitch as the needle punctured your skin and every broken bone when it happened, and then the pain of having it set. I have watched all your bruises fester and swell as they turn from a gross, sickening purple to yellow. I've felt every injury you hid and let heal on its own. I've screamed through the darkness, hoping it all will end one way or another. But most of all, I know about the internal scars, the invisible fearful tremors your heart tries to pump through. The ones you fight against when you lay in bed not able to sleep, the ones that bring the dread pushing away any ounce of hope. The dread of him coming to you, veiled in darkness with his sick and twisted actions he considers love. But it's those same fearful tremors that keep you going. You hold onto them tight because the fear means you're still able to feel something, rely on something. It's your only constant in a dark, silent place. They've replaced any hope you may have had, leaving you with nothing else except them. Don't tell me I don't know you, Clarissa." I let that hang in the room like a belligerent shadow only we can see, willing her to understand and believe I know what I'm talking about. "I don't know where you came from, Clarissa, but I sure as hell know where you'll end up!"

"How can you and your friend help me?" She's crying now and trying to wipe her eye as the tears back up, creating a soggy poultice clinging to her face, inflaming her eye. "Benjamin will kill me before he lets me go, he told me so. But first, he'll take out his anger on my mother; that's if she's even still alive. He hasn't let me speak to her in over ten years." She's silent now, gulping in ragged breaths as she picks imaginary lint from the hospital blanket, flicking the same imaginary lint to the floor. Pulling her knees up, she begins to rock back and forth as she continues. "I'm not allowed to go anywhere by myself, I can't even drive. He buys my clothes, picks out the TV programs I can watch, and even plans the dinner menus for the week then does all the shopping. I have no money or credit cards. I'm not allowed a cellphone or access to the internet. He calls our landline every hour when he's at work to check on me and scrutinizes the phone numbers on the monthly bill. I swear he can hear my thoughts." As her voice begins to escalate with defeat, she continues. "I'm so lost and ashamed, I've quit looking for a way out, so you and your friend don't have to waste your time on me!"

I sit on the edge of the bed and turn my phone onto video and start asking questions. Because our phones are monitored 24/7 by John's security techs back at the Club House, there is an instant record being processed as I continue. "What's his name and date of birth?" She looks at me drained, and doubtful anything could possibly come of this, but answers.

"Benjamin Troy, April 2, 1978." She looks at me and I can tell she's scared to death. I don't have time to calm her down or placate her, I need to move on.

"Where does he work?"

"He's part owner of a landscaping business." Well, that explains the injury excuse and how the shovel comes into play, I think to myself.

"What's the name of the business?"

"Two Guys Landscaping," she says with a sigh. "What does this matter? You won't be able to do anything; he's too smart and controlling." I don't need to see her face to feel the indignity she carries, the overwhelming load that over time keeps getting bigger, heavier. And as the load builds, doing its best to defeat women like us, there comes a slight chaser of clarity. A small spark of resignation all victims eventually face as they fall deeper and deeper into the darkness of despair. It's like a mantra chanting over and over inside a victim's head. *I'm whole but broken, I'm sane but crazy. I'm beaten but not dead, not yet!* I move on like I didn't hear her, we all wear the face of our own demons and carry its nasty burden. We're running out of time.

"Does he have guns or any kind of weapons?"

"I only know of a shotgun and some kind of a small handgun. He made a point of showing them to me when he brought them home. As far as I know, they're still in his gun safe, and I don't know the combination!"

"Does he have any hobbies, does he drink?"

"Yes, there's a bar he goes to, but I don't know where it is, someplace by the business, I think. But it's not alcohol that drives him to destroy me. I think he's just evil; he feeds on power and jealousy! And as far as I know, the only hobby he has is me," she says and winces in pain, touching her jaw tenderly.

"Does he have any family?" I ask.

"No, he lost his mother when he was a boy and never knew his father. He was raised by an uncle who passed on before we met."

"Do you know his uncle's name?"

"No."

"Okay, what about your mother, what's her name? Do you remember a phone number or address?"

"Yes," she says and gives me the information she remembers.

"Okay, that's enough to get started," I say and turn off the video. "Clarissa, I can't explain everything now, but just know this, my friends and I are *very* good at what we do. We have unlimited resources all over the country at our disposal."

"But what about Benjamin's threat against my mom?"

"Clarissa, I promise if you decide to accept our help, we'll find her. We'll make sure she's safe for as long as we need to." She nodded, indicating she had heard me, but at the same time conflicted on whether she could trust me or not. I understand and relate to every conflicting emotion she's feeling. I know how hard it is because she hasn't been able to think or reason for herself in so long. I've walked through those dreaded deliberations and have grown to expect this hesitation from the women we first approach. I definitely understand the conflict she's feeling. This is the norm; she has to weigh the consequences to herself if I can't deliver, or worse yet, betray her. I honestly can't blame her, and my heart breaks watching her cautiously measure her choices.

"Now," I say, "you're going to be here for at least another week, maybe ten days or so. During that time, please think about our conversation but keep this in mind. In order to move forward and leave this hell behind, there are going to be a lot of changes and conditions. You'll have to agree to both with no hesitation or deviation whatsoever. It's not only for your safety but for ours as well. You'll have to leave the state and become someone else. There can be no contact with anyone, not even your mother, until we deem it's safe."

She blinked her eye and looked at me with such loss and confusion. "I don't understand how I got here!"

"Unfortunately, you were destined to end up here the minute you met him. He was looking for you, waiting for you," I say a bit too harshly. I take a deep breath and try to speak calmly. "Will you please think about what I've told you?"

"Yes, thank you," she says. "Can I ask you a question?"

I nod my head and say, "Of course."

"Did your friend help you get out?"

It's an obvious conclusion to draw by looking at me. I still feel so much shame and carry the anger toward my weakness when I relive my escape. The question is expected during this initial contact and asked of me each time. I wear my past as a mask, not having the luxury of removing it to set on a shelf, putting all the sorrow on display elsewhere. The mask is permanent. *I am the face of Mickey.*

"No," I say, "but they put me back together as much as they could." I stand and move a little closer to the head of the bed. "The night this happened"—I indicate to my face with a wavering touch—"fate was the unsung hero that I believe intentionally stepped in and saved my life. My husband was so drunk that night, but he was still able to destroy my body one more time. He was staggering and breathing heavy after the first round did its damage. He had guzzled his last beer and decided to jump in his truck to go get another six-pack. He'd drink it while warming up for round two." I'm watching the scene play out as usual, the imaginary projector rolling the film, portraying the memory above Clarissa's bandaged head. I'd love to be able to edit the reel, cut and splice the film as they say, and do a retake to delete the pain. But I bring my eyes back to her and continue. "The next thing I remember, I was looking into the kind face of a man wearing a Thurston County Sheriff's uniform. It just so happened that my husband wrapped his drunken ass around a telephone pole while speeding down the road to the Liquor Mart. The deputy found me lying in a bloody heap when they had come to my door to deliver the 'bad' news, which turned out to be the best news of my life." I look at her and say, "I understand perfectly now about KARMA being a bitch."

We hear a quick knock on the door, and I go open it a crack peering out. "You better wrap this up, Reggie, my eyes out there tell me the husband is going totally haywire and ready to explode," John whispers.

"OK, one more minute," I tell him. I look at Clarissa holding herself tightly around the middle, rocking back and forth with fear. "It's alright," I say, trying to calm her. "He can't hurt you here. If you choose to trust us, this is what you do. When the cafeteria volunteer comes into your room asking about your dinner order, I want you to request a milkshake, just a milkshake, nothing else, got it?"

"Wait... What? I don't understand!"

"Clarissa, order *ONLY* a milkshake and we'll take it from there, OK???"

"Yes," she whispers.

I turn and open the door. John is waiting and tells me to leave out the same door we came in. I look back one more time at Clarissa and remember all the Clarissas before her. "It's okay, Reggie, I got this," John says and smiles. "Give my best girl a kiss for me."

I return his smile as best I can and turn to leave, but before I do, I stop halfway down the hall and turn back to see him still watching me. "Of course, she'll expect nothing less since she saw you open the door for me downstairs." His concern and fondness for Suzie are so genuine, that I put my wishes in writing for Suzie to go to him if something should ever happen to me.

Chapter 10

As I push through the exit door, I miss a step and land too hard on my right foot, causing pain to zap my knee and do a heavy taser charge up my thigh. I steady myself with a hand on the cold railing and push on, knowing I'll feel worse later. My thoughts have become toxic; they fill my personal space, trying to extinguish all the air from my lungs. They begin to pull me down the rabbit hole, as they always do at this point in our cases. Like Alice in Wonderland, I'm spiraling down to meet the Mad Hatter, but in my Wonderland, the Mad Hatter stands sentry for the pain and darkness that will come again. I try to stop myself from plummeting down the hole, but there's nothing to hold onto. The darkness beckons, pulling me down through its claustrophobic tunnel, squeezing tighter and tighter. The Cheshire Cat waits at the bottom to taunt me with his grin, where his revolting laugh rings through the darkness, screeching like nails on a classroom chalkboard. He steps into the small stream of light that dances through the hole I just tumbled through. Then he grins nastily and turns to indicate the table is set for tea, and once again... I'm the guest of honor.

Suzie is scratching at the window, trying to squeeze through the small opening. She wants to meet me halfway as I dash toward the Explorer. Her anxiety builds as she tries to throw comfort through the crack in the window, where it's meant to attach itself and bring me home. I run to her as if she's my mother, waiting with open arms to hold and reassure me I'm not alone and everything will be okay.

As I drive out of the parking lot, I can feel my heart rate slowing down, and my nerves are beginning to settle a bit. Suzie is watching me intently, her eyes never leaving my face as I reach up to touch her softly. She lets out a soft guttural sound of understanding, then leans over and licks the single tear that has begun to run down my cheek. Her tongue is gentle as it touches my face and I thank her with a small smile. I look over and notice her baby has been stripped of its soft fuzz, the cloth exposed and completely clean. There is wet fuzz lying in colored clumps all over the passenger seat and floor. She uses her babies like a good

Catholic uses Rosary beads to pray in silence while kneeling in front of a pew on Sunday morning, pouring their heart out, asking for forgiveness and guidance. I believe she prays to her own God just as earnestly, but instead of beads, she uses her baby while waiting for me. She rubs it with her paws and licks it nervously while pouring out her own heart for guidance, and the strength to help me as she waits for my return.

As I look at the chaos and havoc she's done in my honor, I wonder. Did I ever pray in my own way? Did I ever pray in any way? And if I did pray, why did I pray? Did I think praying would somehow recapture the strength I once had, or was the praying to finally find the courage to just give up and let the evil finish me? Maybe if I had given my decimated heart over to something I could believe in, I would have done more than just endure the darkness. Maybe, just maybe, I wouldn't have just survived and the self-respect I'd lost would have begun to show signs of life. I truly envy those who find comfort in their beliefs, in something bigger than themselves. But the guilt of surviving my unbelievable horror stops me from being grateful I actually survived. It feeds my shame, making my pity party of losses that much crueler. I carry my scars inside and out as a reminder of how I failed, how I lost my soul and respect of self. I believe our self-respect is a strong emotion that we nurture through life experience as we grow. It isn't a developed trait we are all born with, but a warm glow deep within us. We cultivate it, cherish it, and mold it with strength and a sturdy sense of right and wrong. We encourage its warmth to mature and lead us through life; we individualize it to be an extension of ourselves. But when it's stripped from our hearts and souls by days and months and years of degradation, it can only return if we feel we're worthy. Will we be able to help Clarissa find that small flicker she was born with, the warm glow that was present as she took her first breath? And if she finds it and nurtures it, will she feel she's worthy? Will I ever feel I'm worthy? The one thing I know for sure: I'm still a work in progress. There's a big difference between surviving and being a survivor.

Looking out the window, I realize I'm wandering through side streets adjacent to the hospital, and for a short time, I'm not sure what I should do or where I should go. The burning urge to run and never look back is overwhelming and seems to have a mind of its own. It's taking control of my thoughts and pushing my feelings of hopelessness to their limit, dragging me back down the hill of despair, past the milestones I have worked so hard to conquer.

I hear a concerned whimper from the passenger seat and see a paw reach over to place a heartening understanding on my arm. I am shaken by my old emotions, dragging me back down the hill but am grateful for Suzie's touch and eyes of understanding. I know they will eventually guide me to the same place on that hill, standing among all the accomplishments I have made, reminding me of how far I have come. She has a way of grounding me and helping me focus on what lies ahead, on what we need to do. I decide to pull over and get my thoughts together, put my mental to-do list in order, and hopefully get back up that hill. I always wonder if this will be the time I don't make it, don't manage to get up to reclaim the ground I already conquered. But I have grown enough to know that each time I fall, I manage to get back up on my feet and use the setback as a challenge to push myself even further. It's always a cruel challenge to have to start at the bottom of previous accomplishments, to have to look up and see where you were, then find the resolve once again to begin the long journey in recapturing familiar ground. But it's enlivening when I pass previous hurdles I defeated in the past, stomping my way through old decay to add another foot or two up the hill.

I find my phone and call Abby, who picks up before the first ring even registers in my ear.

"How did it go, Reggie, are you okay?" Abby's concern is heartfelt and honest for both myself and Clarissa. I can feel it through the phone and am so grateful for it and her. Sometimes she grounds me as much as Suzie does.

"Abby, we haven't had one this dark for a long time," I say, sitting in my car, feeling drained and sickened. "She's managed to live and exist in a horrible situation for so long. She has to have a strength she doesn't even know is there." I'm visualizing her claiming a corner in the cellar of defeat, among the others who have arrived before her. She sees the stairs that lead to the door at the top but hasn't acknowledged the light of hope that seeps through the space underneath. Hopefully, if we crack the door open a bit, she'll climb the stairs and push it open further.

"Do you think she'll trust us enough to help her? Michael says we don't have a lot of time, and if she doesn't accept our help, she won't either."

"I don't know at this point. I told her to think it over while she's in the hospital. She knows what to do if she wants our help. Now it's just a waiting game for us while she figures out if she wants to trust us. Her only other option is to not take our help and go back home with him, and unfortunately, he's more dangerous than we imagined."

"Is there anything you need from me while we wait?"

I look at Suzie and the mayhem she has created in my car, so I reach out and scratch the top of her head. She leans into my hand, trying to pull all the internal sorrow I lug around from my touch, pleading with her eyes to let her carry the burden. I look at her face and smile to myself, then look back down on the floor of the car where the pink carnage from her baby lies. "Yes," I say, "Miss Suzie needs a new baby. She has worried this one clean, if you know what I mean. You better make it more than one; if we get the green light on this, Suzie will need a few backups."

"Oh, the poor thing, it's always so hard for her to wait for you, knowing what we're heading into again. Okay, I'll have one of the runners get some from the Club House and bring them to your motel."

"Thank you, Abby, just have him leave them at the front desk. Oh, before I forget, have one of John's techie techs remotely scrub our phones and my laptop of anything concerning Clarissa. Now we have a file on our servers if we need anything in the future. Also, in the meantime, have them use the information on the mother she gave us and try to track her down. If she's still alive, we'll need to have eyes on her the minute we get the green light from Clarissa. If we get the green light, that is."

"Sounds good, honey, remind me again where you're staying?"

With a heavy sigh, I say, "I'm going to tell you, but you have to promise you won't go all June Cleaver on my ass because the Beaver has had a long day!" I wink at Suzie and she winks back, along with an understanding snort. She's always got my back.

"Okay, Beaver, I won't, but Ward isn't going to be very happy," she says with a giggle. "Tell Suzie her babies are on the way."

Chapter 11

We've been here before, the three of us—Suzie, Mickey, and me. We wait to play advocate for someone who may not want it, doing our best to get ready for a horrible tour if we're asked. I reach out and stroke Suzie's good ear, and feel its silky softness begin to calm me. I'm feeling exhausted and helpless, and my leg is throbbing from the misstep I took coming out of the hospital. I begin to move my hand over my knee and up my leg, realizing an ice pack and a handful of ibuprofen are in my future. Sometimes I feel like the Tin Man searching for his oil can—a couple of drops here, a couple of drops there, and all would be good. I already have my heart, even though it's damaged and continually trying to beat itself past the darkness it has known.

I look at Suzie and tell her I love her, and she gives me her best "I know" smile in return. "You do realize you have a crap-tastic mess to clean up, sister," I say and point to the mayhem all over the passenger seat and floor. "But that can wait, let's go get you a new baby." She gives me a happy snort and turns in the seat, happy to ride shotgun on this special mission.

The keeper of the room keys sits behind the counter; she looks up from her book to give me a nod as I push open the door to the office. I think her name is Ruth, but I've never asked. She is a massive woman, who towers over me from behind the counter when she stands. Her hair is short and kinky curly, cupping her head like a frizzy helmet. She is built large at the chest and shoulders, but from the waist down, she is slim. "There should be a package for room 122," I say. She looks at me for a second, trying to visualize the damage that is hidden behind my sunglasses. I think of them as a shield, hiding some of the evidence the human race is capable of. She's never asked, but I get the feeling we have shared something that neither of us want to explore further. She clears her throat and coughs up phlegm from the million and one cigarettes she's polluted her body with over the years.

"The messenger just left," she says and coughs again while retrieving the package. I open the large envelope marked "SUZIE" and pull out one of the new bunnies and lay it on the counter. She looks at me, then eyes the stuffed animal with amusement. "Well, whatever floats your boat, sister," she says, letting out a wheeze as she begins to try and laugh. But instead, another hacking fit ensues so severe it causes me to back up a few steps from the counter, because hell, I didn't know what was going to come flying out. All I can do is wait while she dislodges whatever it is she has stuck in her throat, leaving me slightly nauseous. "Is that for you or your four-legged friend?" she asks more for conversation than real curiosity as she tries again to figure out the story hidden behind my sunglasses. She coughs again, letting the heavy rattle escape through a throat that sounds like it's coated with sandpaper, her tired, overworked lungs doing their best to expel the thick residue of nicotine.

"No, it's not mine," I say. "It's hers." And right on cue, Miss Suzie places her large front paws on the counter, flashing her most charming smile, then grabs her new baby and heads for the door. I turn and pick up the envelope, tuck it under my arm, and make my way to the door as well.

"We do have a policy about pets in the rooms, you know," she wheezes loudly as I open the door for Suzie.

"I know," I say, acknowledging the comment as the door closes behind me. I just smile to myself because she tells me the same thing every time she sees us. I know she doesn't really give a crap about Suzie because she's never pushed it. Anyway, they're highly compensated each time I stay here at the luxurious Motel 6 Ritz. The compensation is for Suzie and the secrecy I'm confident the keeper of the room keys will keep. I'm appreciative of her perceptive and non-intrusive manner of support, so I know we are safe here.

We head to the back of the motel where we have two connecting rooms. When we turn the corner, I notice the three doors before ours are veiled in darkness. I park my car a few doors down from our rooms and step out, telling Suzie to stay close. My brain registers the possibility that the bulbs have been tampered with, making it impossible to read the room numbers and worse. With no light, a person is vulnerable trying to unlock their door. Hopefully, they've just burned out. However, it does seem strange that three bulbs in a row would go out at the same time. I'm on instant alert and wait in the shadows of the huge Arborvitae hedge planted around the parking lot. I look at Suzie with her baby in her jaws and whisper, "Anything?" She becomes rigid beside me as she sniffs the air, her ear standing at attention, but after a few heartbeats, she looks at me and wags her tail. We're safe to head to our room, moving through the darkness that claims the three doors before ours. Most guests would complain about the lack of lighting, but it suits us perfectly once we know it's safe. In fact, when we get to our room, I reach up and loosen the bulb next to our door, making the darkness stretch to four. Then I walk back to the first door covered in darkness to test the bulb. I relax a bit more once I know the bulb is actually burnt out, then check the other two and find they have burned out as well. We are always on alert, even when we aren't currently working. It's become an ingrained habit for all of us because we know in the back of our minds there are a lot of previous dangers out there. Not all of the devil's minions follow the rules and warnings doled out by Mickey!

I open the door to our room and feel the exhaustion hit me like a heavy cloak of emotional gloom, but I can't give in to it just yet. I feed Suzie and give her fresh water before I get comfortable with my ibuprofen and ice pack. I lay on the bed and try to relax, breathing deep, in and out, in and out. I hear the tags on Suzie's collar clang against her dish, and then hear the shower of water she sprays all over as she tries to completely submerge her head in the water dish. One thing about Miss Suzie, she's not a dainty girl. But then again, neither am I. When I was young, my small frame, agility, and strength always gave me a natural athletic ability.

In my senior year of high school, I was on my way to a full-ride girls Fast Pitch scholarship to Gonzaga University. I attributed my strength and focus to pursue that scholarship on the crippled life that was dealt to me through no choice of my own. I never had any stability in all my years growing up. I was looking for some kind of unity, some kind of "got your back" sibling bond that any kind of family, real or not, would provide. I found through high school sports and being part of a team filled that void. But all the honed focus and strength I had was lost the day I met *him*... He took his directions from the Devil, taking his time to find out what it was I craved and offered me that home and promise of a family. Gradually, and very shrewdly, he was able to destroy my strength and focus; I no longer wanted the scholarship or the future it would give me. Without even realizing it, I let him work the Devil's dark magic, so slowly I became dependent on him and stopped thinking for myself. I became an instant addict to his lies; his darkness bled into my soul and I had nowhere to go. Like the first taste of crack, he hooked me, consumed me; I can't believe I was that weak. So just like all the others, I continue to ask myself how I could have let that happen. My guilt continues to be pushed to the limit, and I can't forgive myself for the weakness that took over. He had no one to threaten, no one I cared about to keep me in line. Could I have wanted it in some way? I always thought I had a good head on my shoulders, along with a well-developed bullshit detector. But I didn't see this one coming; my detector had failed me, and I gave my heart to a well-disguised foot soldier for the Devil. For some reason, that I still can't figure out, I made the transformation so easy.

I lay on the bed waiting for the ibuprofen to kick in and focus on the wait ahead of us. The hardest part about waiting is thinking of all the atrocious scenarios we may face, and the unbearable helplessness we know they'll bring. My head begins to spin with the unknown, sending my mind into a journey of questions. I wonder if Clarissa will be leading us into another shit storm, and if she does, what will the heart-wrenching ordeal cost each of us personally. Every rescue we make takes a sad chunk from each of us, but we'll do it again and again because there's always another and another who will need our help. I yawn and rub my eyes, finally feeling my body relax. I adjust the ice pack and feel its coldness work itself into my knee and leg. My body feels the mattress move as Suzie lies beside me, her warm body is welcome, and I let her know that by stroking her fur and murmur a well-deserved, *I love you.* My eyes close and I feel myself drift off.

The cause of my fear is here; he's standing at the foot of my bed. Bright lights shroud his body, casting it as some kind of sterile presence. His head lifts from his shoulders and begins to float toward me with its most sinister sneer; it moves back and forth demanding my silence as he sends me a message. I'm feeling cold and defenseless as the head dances above the bed, hovering closely with its dark eyes roaming my body, determined to make wanted the scholarship or the future it would give me. Without even realizing it, I let him work the Devil's dark magic, so slowly I became dependent on him and stopped thinking for myself. I became an instant addict to his lies; his darkness bled into my soul and I had nowhere to go. Like the first taste of crack, he hooked me, consumed me; I can't believe I was that weak. So just like all the others, I continue to ask myself how I could have let that happen. My guilt continues to be pushed to the limit, and I can't forgive myself for the weakness that took over. He had no one to threaten, no one I cared about to keep me in line. Could I have wanted it in some way? I always thought I had a good head on my shoulders, along with a well-developed bullshit detector. But I didn't see this one coming; my detector had failed me, and I gave my heart to a well-disguised foot soldier for the Devil. For some reason, that I still can't figure out, I made the transformation so easy.

I lay on the bed waiting for the ibuprofen to kick in and focus on the wait ahead of us. The hardest part about waiting is thinking of all the atrocious scenarios we may face, and the unbearable helplessness we know they'll bring. My head begins to spin with the unknown, sending my mind into a journey of questions. I wonder if Clarissa will be leading us into another shit storm, and if she does, what will the heart-wrenching ordeal cost each of us personally. Every rescue we make takes a sad chunk from each of us, but we'll do it again and again because there's always another and another who will need our help. I yawn and rub my eyes, finally feeling my body relax. I adjust the ice pack and feel its coldness work itself into my knee and leg. My body feels the mattress move as Suzie lies beside me, her warm body is welcome, and I let her know that by stroking her fur and murmur a well-deserved, *I love you.* My eyes close and I feel myself drift off.

The cause of my fear is here; he's standing at the foot of my bed. Bright lights shroud his body, casting it as some kind of sterile presence. His head lifts from his shoulders and begins to float toward me with its most sinister sneer; it moves back and forth demanding my silence as he sends me a message. I'm feeling cold and defenseless as the head dances above the bed, hovering closely with its dark eyes roaming my body, determined to make sure I obey his warning. I feel a warm hand touch my arm and hear a voice I don't recognize.

"Mrs. Reynolds," the voice says. "Can you hear me?"

His head is still floating above me, moving back and forth, then up and down, circling the gentle voice I hear. Its dark and deliberate message is delivered with malice.

"Mrs. Reynolds, Regina, I'm so sorry there was too much damage!"

"No, no, no," I mutter over and over, trying to get the voice to stop talking, hoping with all my heart that if I don't hear it, it won't be true. But the voice continues; it travels down a tunnel, fading in and out, but the unbearable words still manage to crash into me like angry swells against a rocky coast.

"We did our best to save your baby but were unsuccessful. Regina, there was too much damage, causing you to bleed internally. We tried to stop the bleeding coming from your uterus but were unsuccessful. That left us only one option, and that was to remove it. I'm so, very sorry." I'm screaming inwardly, looking at the headless dark devil standing at the foot of my bed. He's holding his head in his hands now, extending it out to me as a dark offering. He's letting its eyes do the talking as they continue to rip me apart with multiple warnings, making sure their meaning is clear. But I don't care what the eyes want or insist on, because now he has taken my child as well as my soul. The warm hand is there again; it reaches up and brushes my hair back from my face, wiping the tears from my eyes and cheeks.

"Regina, do you understand? There will be no more pregnancies, no children," the soft voice says in a pained whisper.

I don't want to believe the voice. I want to place my hands up into my womb and search for the only innocence I had. But I know in my heart it is empty of my small miracle, and all it could have been. I mourn for what's missing and grieve for the tiny creation I couldn't protect.

I try to lunge at the devil's soldier; I want to rip him apart and empty his soul like he has emptied mine. I want to hold that soul and its consuming darkness in my hands and squeeze the life out of it. I want it to bleed and scream at the light as it shrinks in on itself, pulling the walls of his being with it. Then slowly, a tiny piece of me acknowledges the comfort in knowing that the Devil will not become a grandfather, or his soldier a father. They can't hurt the missing innocence anymore or have the chance to mold it into a copy of their viciousness. All I have left is emptiness; I'm emptied of any happiness or goodness that could have been. At this moment, I want to join the precious innocent that was ripped from me and sleep in eternal peace.

I can't move; I'm reaching out with my hands to strangle him in the darkness. I'm crying, and kicking and screaming, then silence. My eyes pop open to the furry face of my protector and the gentleness she provides to calm me. She nuzzles my neck with her cold nose, telling me I'm safe.

Chapter 12

I wake in the morning to a whining at the door. Miss Suzie needs her morning constitutional, urgently. I look over at her and remember I didn't take her out after she ate last night, and the guilt slams me like a hammer. "I'm so sorry, Suz, you must be ready to burst." I look for my shoes but realize I still have them on, and my clothes as well; I slept in everything I was wearing yesterday. "UGH!"

When we're done outside and Suzie is fed, I hear my phone ping with a message. "Meeting at the Club House at 11:00 am, bring Gorgeous," followed by 😊😊. I turn to Suz and let her know her best guy is expecting her this morning. I look at the time and note I have a couple of hours yet, plenty of time to shower and find clean clothes. I pop a couple more ibuprofen and get moving.

The Club House is actually a huge hangar; its total dimensions are the same as an NFL football field. The location is perfect, just off of I-5 and mingled amongst a multitude of identical hangars, which are connected to the Sea-Tac Airport for easy access to the runway. Inside the hangar, John's Security Firm takes up a small space in the left front corner. It has a regular access door from the front of the building into the Security Firm office, giving the impression that's what the hangar is used for, and in some ways it is. John still does some private security for a few elite individuals, but just for his original clients. But since Mickey was created, he hasn't taken on anyone new.

90% of John's security techs and field agents work for Mickey. They're made up of ex-military who served overseas and now use their expertise to help Mickey, each one dedicated to their core cause. The middle of the hangar is used for the Club House, leaving the next section for the motor pool and its numerous vehicles used by the surveillance teams.

Then at the far end of the hangar is Mickey's private plane. An Ultra-Luxurious Gulfstream G650, which I have yet to see the inside of, but from the looks of it, we spent some of those zeros Abby was talking about. There's an Emergency/Surgical Department equipped with everything you can think of, including a staff consisting of doctors, nurses, X-ray techs as well as PT specialists. The ER is staffed 24 hours a day for the security details in the field, as well as the rest of us, including Suzie, whose vet is always on call. There's a workout area for lifting weights, strength training, and physical therapy used by us and our rescues. In one corner of the workout area is a batting cage, which I use more than anyone else. It's how I let off steam, keep my muscles toned, and work up some full-blown cardio. I find it works as therapy for my burnt-out soul as well. We have a well-stocked kitchen and laundry room equipped with the latest appliances. A bunkhouse with a dozen beds on one wall plus a bathroom and a shower on the other. There's a private bedroom and bathroom off of that for the rescued. We are working 24/7, 365, so it is a comfortable place for our techs to grab some sleep and a shower. Up a flight of metal stairs, just past the bunkhouse and circling the perimeter, is a jogging track. We members of Mickey use it to stay in shape and encourage the rescues to add cardio to their PT when they are strong enough. In many cases, and Clarissa will be one, *may be one*, we need to follow the doctors' orders before we can proceed with the transition into their new life. They need to become strong and focused before making their decisions as to where they want to go and what they access to the runway. Inside the hangar, John's Security Firm takes up a small space in the left front corner. It has a regular access door from the front of the building into the Security Firm office, giving the impression that's what the hangar is used for, and in some ways it is. John still does some private security for a few elite individuals, but just for his original clients. But since Mickey was created, he hasn't taken on anyone new.

90% of John's security techs and field agents work for Mickey. They're made up of ex-military who served overseas and now use their expertise to help Mickey, each one dedicated to their core cause. The middle of the hangar is used for the Club House, leaving the next section for the motor pool and its numerous vehicles used by the surveillance teams.

Then at the far end of the hangar is Mickey's private plane. An Ultra-Luxurious Gulfstream G650, which I have yet to see the inside of, but from the looks of it, we spent some of those zeros Abby was talking about. There's an Emergency/Surgical Department equipped with everything you can think of, including a staff consisting of doctors, nurses, X-ray techs as well as PT specialists. The ER is staffed 24 hours a day for the security details in the field, as well as the rest of us, including Suzie, whose vet is always on call. There's a workout area for lifting weights, strength training, and physical therapy used by us and our rescues. In one corner of the workout area is a batting cage, which I use more than anyone else. It's how I let off steam, keep my muscles toned, and work up some full-blown cardio. I find it works as therapy for my burnt-out soul as well. We have a well-stocked kitchen and laundry room equipped with the latest appliances. A bunkhouse with a dozen beds on one wall plus a bathroom and a shower on the other. There's a private bedroom and bathroom off of that for the rescued. We are working 24/7, 365, so it is a comfortable place for our techs to grab some sleep and a shower. Up a flight of metal stairs, just past the bunkhouse and circling the perimeter, is a jogging track. We members of Mickey use it to stay in shape and encourage the rescues to add cardio to their PT when they are strong enough. In many cases, and Clarissa will be one, *may be one*, we need to follow the doctors' orders before we can proceed with the transition into their new life. They need to become strong and focused before making their decisions as to where they want to go and what they want to do. Each woman is brought to the Club House only after I've spent time with them and am absolutely sure they aren't going to run. We can't take the chance of our location being revealed. Finally, in the center of the hangar is the heart of Mickey. Its soft lighting hangs from open rafters and metal pipes, mixing their soft glows with the harsh lighting of hundreds of computer screens. The screens hum with real-time info, alerting the dedicated techs standing vigil with second-by-second updates. Their diligence protects every member of our team, as well as the hundreds of individuals and their families we have helped in the past if we feel it's still needed. The monitoring of the past is just as important as the monitoring of the present.

The dedicated monitoring of all parties involved immediately after an extraction is major. A current rescue needs to be assured she is safe as she spins on a carousel of life-changing decisions. And even when the spinning reverses and she finds herself still clinging to the past, riding the old carousel of helplessness, she will know she's protected. Our goal is to get the spinning to reverse again, so she can choose from the kaleidoscope of possibilities waiting. We want her to eventually pick a future and exit into a new life with power and confidence. We all know our techs' unrelenting dedication to their safety helps form the foundation for making that exit happen.

Every time I walk in, I'm reminded of that television series with Kiefer Sutherland, *24,* with all the activity, lighting, and phones ringing. All we need is Jack Bauer screaming, "We're running out of time, get me that visual now!" So, as Suzie and I enter, I see our own version of Jack Bauer coming our way. Suzie is excited to see John and bounds forward as he kneels down for a kiss. "There's my best girl," he says while accepting all of Suzie's kisses. He looks at me and stands, stating the obvious. "You look like crap, and why are you limping? You need to see the doc right now," he says with a stern but concerned voice.

"Good morning to you too, John," I say sarcastically. "I tweaked my leg when I missed a step coming out of the hospital door yesterday. I'm on my way to have it checked out now. Will you keep Suz occupied for a bit?"

"Of course," he says and snags a treat out of a container from the nearest desk. Every desk has its own treat bowl, and Suzie knows it. She will manage to make the rounds in the Club House before she leaves, and not just to say hello. I may be the face of Mickey, but Suzie is the Club House mascot.

I turn my head as I'm walking away. "Hey, John, will you have a tech from the motor pool sweep my car before I leave?" Our mindset is, we can't be too careful; we never know if we could have been compromised, so checking for monitoring devices isn't overkill by any means.

"Will do," he says and gives me a salute, which is something the real Jack Bauer would never do. "When you're done, meet us in the conference room." I give him the thumbs up and continue walking, more like limping, to the medical bay.

Chapter 13

As I walk toward the conference room, I'm greeted by Suzie, who looks like she's been having a great time checking in with all the techs. She falls into step beside me as I push open the heavy glass door and enter a room full of concerned eyes, all waiting for me to hopefully put their minds at ease. "X-rays are good, just some muscle strain," I explain to everyone seated around the huge conference table. Michael is relieved and tells me so. Abby is seated next to him and smiles, as always, her portable laptop in front of her. I sit down next to John, and Suzie takes up the space between us. There is a tray of sandwiches and fruit in the center of the table, and my stomach growls when I look at it. Suzie is eyeing the tray as well, and John is eyeing Suzie eyeing the tray. He leans forward, reaching for half a sandwich, and I stop him. "That better be for you, John, because Suzie already had her breakfast. And I'm guessing she's had a treat from every desk out there as well," I say, pointing through the glass walls of the conference room. "But I haven't eaten yet, so don't mind if I do." I reach for the tray, trying unsuccessfully to avoid the sad, pitiful eyes at my left, and I don't just mean Suzie's.

"Kinda rude, isn't it, gorgeous?" John mutters in Suzie's direction, to which she responds with an "affirmative snort" back at him. She can be such a traitor sometimes, especially where her stomach is concerned.

I look up from my sandwich and see Doc Xander heading our way, still wearing his white lab coat. He's a good-looking man and very dedicated to Mickey's cause. He sits down to my right and hands me a pill bottle. "These will help with the pain, but not knock you off your game, Reggie," he says and smiles. I smile back and tuck the bottle into my coat pocket.

"We've been kicking around some ideas on how to retrieve Clarissa if we're contacted," Michael says. "If she contacts us while still in the hospital, our trusted personnel are on alert and ready for their schedule changes. Everyone is on board, including Xander," Michael indicates with a nod in Doc's direction.

Retrievals are always dangerous; that's why each case needs to be scrutinized and assessed for the worst-case scenario. Our main goal is to complete the extraction as quietly and swiftly as possible for the protection of everyone. It's never easy, and we never have a foolproof plan, but we've been doing this for a while now and have acquired the ability to improvise at the spur of the moment when needed. Even with that going for us, unfortunately, we can't think of everything that could go wrong, so we rely on each of our individual strengths and never get so caught up that we take chances we shouldn't.

John leans forward and adds, "But if she leaves the hospital without contacting us, we need to decide how to proceed from there. We all know she'll go home, and she told us her husband has weapons in his safe. At this point, we have eyes on him around the clock and have placed a GPS tracker on his truck, so we know when he is and isn't at the house. I also think we should at least plant a phone somewhere in or around the house, just in case. If our eyes see any trouble, we can figure out a way to contact her. Let her know we're still here, and she should call. I want to continue monitoring the husband's activities for a while if she does decide to go home with him." Everyone sitting around the table agrees with John, including myself.

"So, you're going back into the field, are ya, Doc?" I say, throwing a wink his way with my good eye. He loves this part of his job as much as he loves his calling. He's an excellent actor, too.

"Absolutely. I can't let you three have all the fun," he says and points to the three of us to his left. "I want to see that piece of shit lose his mind when he realizes he's lost control of her and the situation. We all know that once the object of his control is gone, his world is going to spin hard and fast. Maybe he'll off himself from the loss or get run over in the parking lot while in a frenzied rage. Hell, maybe I'll drive the car personally. In this circumstance, my oath of 'Do No Harm' won't be tarnished in the least, and I'll still sleep like a baby. But for now, let's just focus on getting that woman out of there if we can." He stands now and glances at each of us with determined and hopeful eyes. "Just let me know how you want me to play it when the time comes," then he turns and leaves the room. Silence dances in the space around us as we all nod in agreement. Wow, it's obvious something has hit home with him on this case.

"Well put," Abby whispers, more to herself than the rest of us.

Watching Doc leave, I wonder again what his story is, why he's here with Mickey. One of the unspoken rules within the Club House is you don't ask anyone about their story. Stories as to why each of us is here are protected and sheltered by each individual. We all have our own sad baggage and can choose to share, or not, but we never ask. Even my story is still closed for the most part. One reason I'm here is harshly displayed all over my face. But I leave it up to each individual to try and interpret my dark novel. I believe my chapters are hidden within a sinister narrative only I have the right to interpret.

I clear my throat and look across the table at Abby, "Have we been able to track down Clarissa's mother yet?"

"Yes," she says. "She's still in the same town Clarissa grew up in but is living in an Alzheimer's facility. She's been there for the past five years. The woman I spoke with told me her illness has advanced in the last year or so, and she's slipping downhill rapidly. Maybe if we could give that information to Clarissa, it would help her with her decision. I know if it were me, I'd want to see her to at least say goodbye, whether I was going to be recognized or not."

I nod my head in agreement with Abby, even though I don't know what it's like to have a mom. "Damn it, Clarissa is getting bitch-slapped from every direction; is she ever going to catch a break?"

I ask no one in particular. "John, do we have guardians posted there yet?"

"Yes, I sent a team out there the minute we found her."

"Okay, it's only been one day since I spoke with her, so we still have some time for her to contact us. Michael, how's she doing today?"

"She still needs a lot of medication for her pain, which in a way is good because it also helps her sleep, so healing is progressing nicely. I think she asks for more each time she wakes because if she's asleep, she doesn't have to deal with her husband. We've all seen the worst of mankind in the past years, but he is the classic definition of evil!" He looks at me and knows I understand what he means because I rode that same dark train for many years. It was like riding an out-of-control bullet, shooting me down the tracks toward my dark destiny. I had to endure the tremors in my body, waiting for the conductor to announce, "You're the last stop, Lady, welcome to Hell."

"Do you think all that medication is stopping her from recalling my visit? I mean if she's sleeping so much, she might not remember she has a decision to make. We can't throw her a lifeline if she doesn't know it's a possibility, or what she has to do to catch it."

Chapter 14

John and I hang back and wait for everyone to leave the conference room. We'll use this time while waiting to hear from Clarissa to discuss previous cases and their current monitoring. "Your car was clean," John says as he stands and moves to the door. I follow his gaze and see Zee strolling in with a wide, sleepy grin. "Welcome back, brother," John says and pulls him into a "man" hug. "How does it feel being a new dad?"

"Exhausting as hell, man. I have no idea what I'm doing or what I'm supposed to be doing. Thank God for Beth, because the little thing wouldn't have a chance if he just had me to rely on."

"Congratulations, Zee," I say and reach out my hand. "I hope his name isn't 'Little Thing,' however."

Laughing, he responds, "No, it's James, after my father."

"Well, hopefully, you'll be able to stay awake long enough to fill us in on the two cases you emailed me about," John says. "I'm glad to see that your backup was on top of things as usual."

"Coffee helps immensely," he says with a yawn. He sits down and places two files on the table, opening the top one. "You guys remember Joss McMillian," he states and pulls out two 8x10 photos, pushing them across the table to us. The first picture is of Joss McMillian right before we stepped in to help extract her from her boyfriend, her face battered and beaten almost unrecognizable. The second picture is also of Joss, but with reconstructive changes that not only repaired injuries but her appearance as well. The facial reconstruction was the result of two intricate plastic surgeries, each one leaving her to endure months of painful recovery. I remember that pain all too well, and the long days of recovery, waiting for a miracle that, for me, never came. I'm glad to see the pain and torture was worth it for her; she's beautiful. I hope she is enjoying her new life and identity to the fullest. Looking up, I tell him with my eyes and a slight nod of my head to continue.

"Her rescue took place three years ago," he continues. "For the first two and a half years, we watched over her, her family, and the boyfriend 24/7, using the usual protocols. Six months ago, we dropped the guardian detail and surveillance teams because he hadn't done anything to suggest he was going to be a threat to any of them, no red flags at all. We thought he had gotten the message and we were going to be able to celebrate another success story. But last week, the techs that monitor social media blogs pertaining to domestic violence picked up on a comment that mentioned the boyfriend. So, the team followed our safety guidelines and protocols to find out who the blog belonged to."

"Is it Joss?" Both John and I ask in unison.

"Close, it belongs to her sister. We reached out to her via instant messaging and also her blogger email; she had some very alarming information to pass on. Apparently, he has a new girlfriend, and she has no idea what he's capable of."

I reach out and touch the first photo that portrays a face destroyed by rage. "I think this girl needs to see firsthand what her new boyfriend is capable of and what he'll eventually do to her." I look at John and say, "We need to get a team on the way and arm them all with this photo. Obviously, we'll need to keep eyes on him once she's contacted and sees the picture. At this point, we don't know how either one of them will react or what they'll do. Hell, our good intentions could speed up her fate in one of two ways. Either she'll listen to us and break it off, or not believe us at all and become his second victim." And yes, in this instance, it is that black and white; we know because we've dealt with this guy before.

"I agree," Zee says. "Hopefully, we can shut this guy down fast and save that girl from ending up like this," he says, touching the first photo.

"Looks like this guy's going to need a tune-up," John says. "Why is it some of these guys just don't listen?"

"They don't listen because our messages aren't delivered strongly enough," I say with a hardness they've both heard before. "Jesus, John, all you guys are ex-military; you should know how to deliver pain without actually killing the sucker!" My outburst is received by two pairs of compassionate eyes, each pair showing their own levels of understanding, and both falling short by miles. My reaction is nothing new; they both know I'm not being malicious or condescending, so they sit in silence and watch me chase my demons. As they watch, they're slapped in the face with an open-handed reality. They are reminded again that they will never understand the depth of my pain. I hear a whine and feel Suzie lick my hand, her intent to try and calm me. I turn my head, looking into her concerned eyes, and tell her I'll be fine. "I'm sorry, guys, I know you know what to do," I say with defeat. "I just get so frustrated when we end up moving backward instead of forward. I wish that just once our messages could match the destruction these guys wield, allowing us to turn the tables of violence against them. They need to feel what it's like to be a victim; that's what our messages need to deliver."

So, here we are again, in a reverse time warp, waiting for the condescending dance we have to endure every time we fail. This time, the horned Devil has taken on the persona of a magical Puppet Master, doing a nasty Two Step across the stage of positive ground we thought we'd covered. He wants us to watch as he mends the few strings we severed of Joss's chosen puppet, all the while dancing in the decay he allows to fester on his stage. He knows the puppet in his hands will recover quickly, and he's giddy with the knowledge. He loudly croons his sinister laugh with the music, directing it across the stage to dance with the other puppets that wait for their chance to shine. But when the music stops and the devil bows, we must wait for the never-ending smugness he delivers with the encore of all encores. Smiling, he looks out to us and winks, taunting us with the knowledge that we will never be able to shut him down. He'll never be stopped and will continue to send his army of dark puppets to do his bidding. His army marches on their puppet strings in numbers we will never be able to fathom. Now we need to regroup, learn from our mistakes, and use that knowledge moving forward. God, I get so exhausted watching the same show over and over again, having to sit through the curtain calls of failure.

A sad silence overwhelms the room as we sit like three strangers in a strange land, surrounded by glass walls. These two wonderful men sitting with me have to see into my horrors in order to understand where I'm coming from, and they do it willingly. I feel enormous regret that they have to deal with my past as much as I do; it sickens me deeply. I'm hopeful that someday I'll find myself again, and they can look through the glass walls and just see a strong woman who can say, "I not only survived, I'm a survivor," and not the reluctant hero of Mickey I consider myself to be now. The reluctance stems from the fact that on the night of my emancipation from hell, I had, as usual, handed my fate over to my husband and a case of empty beer bottles. Ironically and sadly, those empty beer bottles set in motion my physical freedom as well as constant regret and suffocating guilt. The truth is, I'm not worthy of the label "hero" in any sense of the word. God knows I did nothing to help myself get here, sitting in this room with so many lives depending on me, on us to help them. After all this time, guilt still rears its ugly head to laugh at me, to remind me of my weakness. But I continue to fight for the day, the hour, and the minute I will forgive myself. Maybe it will be tomorrow, or maybe next week, but I'll keep rebelling against the guilt, and someday, I'll be free, and someday, I will be… a… Survivor.

Zee clears his throat and smiles, trying to lighten the mood. "We do have a success story here," he says. He pulls the second file out, opening it so he can display another photograph. I remember that face and smile. Her name was Nikki Mathews. She was—no, is—an amazingly strong person. I say her name "was" Nikki because I don't want to know where she went, or who she has become. Just like

Joss, once our rescues leave, they are strangers to me. They live a new life, reborn from hard work and sacrifice, in order to move on. I knew she'd make it; I had no concerns once she left to start over, and apparently, I was right. Zee continues, "She and everyone connected to her have followed the safety protocols to the letter. Even the husband is following the rules; he took Mickey's message to heart, seriously. He literally does nothing but go to work and then goes home. The only time he deviates from that routine is on Sunday morning when he goes to the grocery store. I feel good about suggesting we pull the details from this one."

Chapter 15

It's now been four days, and we still haven't heard from Clarissa. Michael is the only one who has seen her, and that's only because he's her doctor. He can't come right out and ask her if she's made a decision without putting himself and the hospital in danger. He did tell her yesterday that she would be able to go home soon if the final X-rays showed the healing to her face was progressing and her eyesight kept improving. He hoped, by giving her that information, she would realize she needed to make a decision, and soon.

I'm doing what I always do when getting antsy: working through some overdue therapy in the batting cage. My session starts out slow as my muscles get warmed up, and I smile because it feels so good to hit something over and over again. Now that I'm warmed up, I move back to a spot on the floor that I know is 35 feet from the pitching machine. I pick up the small remote that controls the machine and set the speed the ball will come at me, then punch in how many seconds I want in between pitches. I grip the only item I took from my old life, my Easton aluminum bat. Its length and drop weight are still perfect for my size. It feels good in my hands, reminding me I'm in control now. Yes, it's the same bat, and I don't give a rat's ass what a shrink would say about it! I take my stance over the imaginary plate and adjust my helmet, watching the digital seconds count down on the screen as I wait for the pitch. Here it comes, and I'm ready, but I swing up, sending the ball foul to my left. The mesh enclosure grabs it with a soft whoosh and rolls it back toward the pitching machine. "Crap," I say, looking at the bat. I inch forward a bit, crowding the imaginary plate and watching the digital seconds count down one more time. Three... two... one. I swing hard, and once again, the ball flies up and foul. "Crap, Crap, Crap!" I scream, stomping my feet in frustration as I glare at the bat like it betrayed me... AGAIN!!!

"It's not the bat's fault, Reggie," John says, laughing, "you're dropping your shoulder again, Slugger."

"I don't need any pointers from the peanut gallery, John. I have yet to see you get in here and back up all your big talk. Isn't that right, Suz?" I say while adjusting my helmet and getting ready for the next pitch. Suzie is my biggest fan and, as always, agrees with me. She's my devoted cheerleader as she sits outside the cage where she's protected, giving me encouraging snorts and barks as I hit.

"Well, if you'd share the cage a little more often, I could show you a thing or two. Fortunately for you, your schooling is just going to have to wait for another day; Clarissa just ordered her milkshake. So, grab a shower and meet us in the conference room in thirty."

"Thank God, I thought we'd lost her before we even got started," I say, taking off my batting glove and shutting everything down. "But, John, when this is over, you're going to get in this cage and back up that big mouth of yours. I think you brag too much to actually be any good." He disregards my comment and walks away laughing.

Suzie and I are the last ones to enter the conference room, and she makes a beeline directly to John, as usual, for his devoted affection. I sit down next to him and watch Suzie head around the table, stopping at each chair for the doting attention she feels she deserves, loving their lavish praise. All faces are familiar to her except one: the tiny woman sitting next to Xander. She stops in front of the chair of the stranger and sits, scrutinizing the woman earnestly, then finally smiles and barks, putting her paw up to shake. John leans over and introduces me and Suzie to Pixie, who happens to be the newest member of Mickey.

"Welcome to the Club House, Pixie," I say, reaching over to shake her hand. She accepts my hand with an affirmative nod and smiles. She is small in stature and very fit. Her hair is blonde and cut short on the sides and back of her head, with longer bangs touching her eyebrows. She has large, blue eyes accented by long lashes and a cute smile. I wonder if Pixie is her real name or a nickname because she really does look like a tiny fairy.

"I hope I can help, Reggie, I'm eager to get started."

"Pix was one of the best snipers in the military," John says, smiling. "She saved many asses when she served under my command, including mine."

Xander stands and fills in some more blanks by saying, "Pixie has just joined the staff at the hospital and will be helping us with Clarissa's extraction." When he's done explaining Pixie's presence, he begins rubbing his hands together with excitement. "I'm thinking Dr. Thadius will be perfect for this part." We all start laughing as his excitement is like that of a kid with a new bike. Xander has developed the Dr. Thadius character to portray the nerd of all nerds, and he plays him well. Dr. Thadius wears heavy dark-rimmed glasses and speaks with a lisp, making it almost impossible to understand him. The last time Xander used Dr. Thadius, he had added some 1970's polyester high-water pants the color of a ripe pumpkin. Their waistband was hiked up to just under his armpits, leaving the hem of the pants to be about four inches too short above his shoes. He wore his black hair slicked back with a ton of product, making it look hard and greasy.

"Oh no, Pixie, you are in for a treat," I say, telling her I'm sorry in advance and shaking my head with condolences. It's good to see Doc's mood has changed since the last time we all met; maybe this is what he needed to come out of his funk.

"Yeth, I can be very thexthy when I wanth to be, so look out," Xander says with his lisp.

"Oh my God, SERIOUSLY!" Pixie laughs while looking at all of us around the table.

"SERIOUSLY!!!!!" we all respond in unison.

"We've had surveillance in place at their home and in Clarissa's hospital room from the very beginning. After she told us about his safe and the guns it holds, we snuck in one night and placed a small camera in the light fixture hanging from the ceiling. It's not the best angle, but we'll be able to see if he opens the safe. In addition, we'll continue the around-the-clock eyes on Benjamin Troy and the monitoring of the GPS tracker on his truck," Marko, our surveillance guru, explains. "We also placed the same kind of camera in the smoke detector in Clarissa's hospital room, which is directly above the television. Her bed faces the wall the television and smoke detector are mounted on, so we're able to have eyes on her every minute also."

Once he explained all the surveillance we had in place, he turned and asked no one in particular to dim the lights while he picked up a small remote. He points to the television screen mounted on the wall behind him and brings up surveillance video of Clarissa's hospital room. The time stamp is ticking away in the bottom left corner of the screen, showing us it's real-time. We all watch and can feel Clarissa's fear jump into the camera, catapulting onto the screen in front of us. It's misery in motion when we see Benjamin Troy walk in and sit down in the chair next to her bed. He doesn't touch her, say, or do anything except keep a heavy stare projected her way. We can all see her body language as it tightens up like a rusted industrial spring holding her fear within its coils. It wants so badly to uncoil and turn her fear into a weapon of rage lashing out at him. She knows he's there, daring her to look at him, but keeps her head turned to the window in a small show of defiance. The only movement he makes is to lift a cup of coffee to his lips, and when he is sipping the hot brew, Marco freezes the video. "This, ladies and gentlemen, is our Trojan Horse. This is how we make a block of time where we can do our extraction."

"By serving him coffee, Marco?"

"No, Reggie, by 'drugging' his coffee. You see, when Dr. Lisp over there and his new sidekick go into Clarissa's room to talk to her and Benjamin, they can tell him she needs one last X-ray before she can be released. I have watched every minute of feed since the beginning of this surveillance detail, and the man is never without a cup of coffee from the cafeteria. The best part is, they don't supply lids for their cups. So, while Xander is distracting him with a lisp here and a lisp there, Pix can do a sleight of hand and drop some kind of knock-out drops into his cup."

"He's right about the coffee," Michael says. "I don't think I've ever seen him without a cup in his hand. We could probably knock him out for a good three hours, and when he wakes up, he'll just think he fell asleep while waiting for Clarissa to get back to the room."

"And if I can't do a 'sleight of hand,' as Marco puts it, what's the backup plan?" Pixie asks, looking around the table. "We do have a backup plan, right?"

"Well, it would have to be the same plan minus the nap," I say. "She'll still need to be taken to X-ray, but without the nap, our time frame for getting her out of there will be tight. I'm thinking we can keep him from getting suspicious for about an hour to an hour and a half. But don't worry, Xander knows how to play it. He'll keep Benjamin distracted in a way that you'll be able to spike the coffee. Right, Dr. Thadius?"

"'Thath' right."

"So, are we all agreed it's a go for tomorrow morning then?"

"Yes," Michael says with concern, "the sooner the better. Pixie, I want you at the hospital by 4:00 am. Benjamin usually isn't there that early, so you can let Clarissa know what's happening and what we need her to do. We can get her discharge papers signed then, saving us time once she's wheeled out of the room. Don't leave her side once Benjamin arrives, and don't drug him too soon; wait for Xander to give you a signal. Also, Xander, give her the medication she'll need to put him out before she leaves today. Any questions?"

"Yes, I have a question." Abby says. "I can only imagine what she's thinking right now. I mean, she ordered the milkshake this morning and must be going crazy, not knowing what's happening. I mean, does she have to sit in the dark until morning, wondering if we got her message?"

I look over Marco's head at the screen and ask him if this is still a live feed. He shakes his head yes, and we all continue to watch. After about five agony-endured minutes of watching, we see Benjamin get up, throw his coffee cup in the trash, and walk out. "THERE!" I say and grab my phone, scrolling through my contacts for the phone number to the hospital. "What room number, Michael?" When the switchboard picks up, I ask for the room number and wait for what seems like an eternity. We all watch the screen as Clarissa is the star of her own black-and-white horror film. She jumps when the phone rings, its shrillness obviously startling her, but after a quick glance at the door where she expects to see her deranged co-star, she picks up the phone.

"Hello," she whispers, and I put her on speaker.

"Clarissa, it's Reggie. We got your message and are working on a plan to get you out of there in the morning. A new nurse will be there early and fill you in on everything. Please don't worry, we're watching Benjamin, and he can't hurt you anymore. Clarissa, he's going to be physically out of your life soon, I promise." The visible relief we see on the screen is heart-wrenching, to say the least. We watch Clarissa hang up the phone with trembling hands, hands that still wear scars, but have begun to heal. I just hope the rest of her can heal as well, but I know from personal experience it's going to take a lot of oil to help that spring begin to uncoil.

"Good call, Abby," I say as I put down my phone. Then turning to John, I ask, "Who do you have to watch my back tomorrow night?"

Chapter 16

I'm up early the next morning, trying to soothe Suzie's worries about today, letting her know she'll be my backup, but she'll have to wait in the car while I go get Clarissa. She is already stressing as she sees me pack our belongings and set them by the door. With her baby in her mouth, she paces back and forth in front of the bags, letting me know she's ready, but as usual, doesn't like the plan. Whether we're successful or not, the bags need to be packed because it's time for Suzie and me to find a new temporary home. This is our normal routine when the time has come to pull someone out. Assuming the extraction goes as planned, I'll bring Clarissa directly back here for the night. This is where the enormity of what she has done will hit her on a scale worse than anything she could have imagined, causing her to have second thoughts no matter how determined we are to help her. Her night will be brutal and terrifying; ours will consist of waiting to see what she decides to do and hoping we can dim the lights on the Puppeteer's stage one more time. Tonight, she may choose to go back—it's happened to us before—and all we can do is watch the mistake take shape. The darkness will come lurking to invade her thoughts, creating a fog of apprehension while setting in motion a mental shakedown of unease. Tonight will be full of emotional deliberation for her; she'll be terrified to go back and terrified to stay. She knows if she goes back, what's in store for her, but has no idea what to expect if she stays, each scenario as disturbingly horrifying as the other. This is why I won't take her directly to the Club House after extraction. We can't compromise its location or our people by opening ourselves up to vulnerability in any way. At this point, Suzie and I are the only ones compromised; that's why I'm packed and ready to bail if she chooses to leave us during the night.

It's time to head to the hospital, and I'm feeling just as jumpy as Suzie at this point. A text from John informs me he'll be at the maintenance department door waiting, just like before. He comes out to meet me as I park the Explorer, informing me that we'll head up the stairs and wait in the same small room where I originally met Clarissa.

"Does Marco have the feed set to send to our phones?"

"Just about. Should be able to pull it in by the time we get upstairs," John says. Before I can give Suzie a pep talk and close the door, he reaches in and gives her a big hug. "She'll be okay, Suzie," John promises, "I have her back." She whines and tries to give him her soggy baby, "No, you keep your baby because she needs you."

We pass through the door and climb up the two levels of steel stairs, then go through the door into the hallway. Just like before, we head directly to the room next to the X-ray Department, quietly slipping in and closing the door. It seems a bit larger this time because there is no bed taking up space. We both grab our phones and are instructed on how to pull in the feed from Clarissa's room. I sit in the plastic chair in the corner, and John chooses to lean up against the door as the feed comes through. We watch Clarissa and Pixie interact while they're waiting for Benjamin and Xander to arrive. Clarissa hands Pixie an envelope, which she folds and slips into her scrub top pocket. I can see Pixie has a gentle touch and way about her. The screen in my hand may be small, but the size doesn't hinder their interaction at all. She is sitting on the edge of Clarissa's bed, leaning in close to try and calm her.

"Shouldn't Benjamin be here by now?" I ask without taking my eyes off my phone. Just then, John's text message tone sings out, and I look up and watch him read it.

"Matt is Benjamin's tail today," John says and lifts his eyes to me. "He said Benjamin just arrived."

We wait in silence for a few minutes, monitoring our screens, my leg jumping, and John's jaw clenching. I decide to try and lighten the mood, so I clear my throat to get his attention. When he looks at me, I give him as much of a smile as I can with the undamaged side of my face. "So, how does a tiny little thing like Pixie end up in Iraq, being that she's so adorable and all?"

"She's not so adorable with an M110 Semi-automatic sniper rifle in her little hands," he laughs and glances back down at his phone. "We started calling her Pixie the minute she joined the unit because, as you can see, she looks just like a woodland fairy from a Disney movie. But after she showed us how well she could shoot, we shortened Pixie to Pix because she just loved to 'pick' off the bad guys one by one to protect the unit. She rotated out after her four years were up. Her family was having some issues, and she was needed at home. When I left to do my last tour, I heard she took her GI Bill and used it to acquire her nursing degree. When I got back, I reached out, and we met for drinks."

"So, you guys hooked up?"

"No, it was just to catch up; no sparks for either of us. She confided in me as to the reason for coming home, though. Her family had lived through a horrible time. So, when I found out by accident that she was joining the staff here, Dad and I felt comfortable approaching her with the idea of joining Mickey as well."

"So, she's got a story," I say sadly. I don't need to remind myself that my story is why I'm sitting with sunglasses and a hood on in the middle of a hospital room. I know I can't hide behind their darkness, but the barriers seem to help me function, at least for now.

"Yes, she has a story. We all have a story, right, Reggie?" I can feel his beautiful green eyes zero in on me as he turns a statement into a question. He's relentless as he tries one more time to get me to open up, hoping this will be the time. But he can't ask me directly without betraying the respect he has for the Club House's unwritten rule not to. Damn, he thinks that if I tell my story out loud, I will be miraculously healed—what a load of crap that is.

"Anyway, it's good there were no sparks firing off between us. Suzie would never be comfortable sharing all this with anyone else." He's animated now, flexing his arm muscles to the max. Their bulging mass stretches the material around his bicep tighter and tighter while turning this way and that like a Mr. Universe competitor. "Besides, I only have eyes for Suzie; she's my best girl."

"Oh my God, John, do you realize how pathetic it sounds that your girlfriend is a dog, literally a dog? Dude!"

"Well, I do now that I said it out loud, damn!"

Chapter 17

"What's taking that Ass Face so long to get up to the room??? Clarissa is totally freaking out!"

"Reggie, try to dial it down a notch. Hopefully, he's getting coffee," John says.

"I will if you will!" I snap back at him. Looking up, I apologize for the outburst, but he's seen worse hostility rear its ugly head within me and just waves me off.

A few more agonizing minutes tick off in the lower left corner of my screen, and I feel like screaming. But a few seconds later, Benjamin walks in, and with great anticipation for things to get moving, I stand and take a deep breath, watching my screen closely. Not quite screaming, but with a raised voice, I start to laugh. "He's here, and he has a cup of coffee! Marco, you wonderful little techie genius, you were right! Now all we need is Dr. Thadius!"

No matter how many times we do this, struggling to keep it together as a plan is playing out is taxing, and waiting for Xander to appear is ramping up the already elevated stress level to new heights. When he does appear a few seconds later, he's sporting the complete Dr. Thadius persona, right down to the high-water pants. He stops at the door like he's waiting to hear the words "ACTION" and then makes an exaggerated, agonizing production of entering the room and pushing the button directly inside the door to dispense the hand sanitizer. While cleansing his hands in an overacting manner, he glances up to the camera and winks. We both laugh out loud as we notice Pixie trying to keep a straight face while moving quickly to position herself behind Benjamin's chair. Now, Xander is heading directly over to Clarissa, where he will begin playing the role that will earn him an Oscar, but only in his own mind, of course. He goes around the bed so he can be positioned on the other side, facing Benjamin, who is clutching Clarissa's hand in a left-handed vice grip. We've watched enough of this horror film over the past week to know that if there's anyone else in the room, Benjamin latches onto either her arm or hand with a controlled warning to be silent. Xander knows this and begins using exaggerated hand gestures to introduce himself before leaning across the bed with his hand reaching out for Benjamin to shake it. Xander is betting that Benjamin won't let go of Clarissa with his left hand, so in order for their hands to connect, Benjamin will have to leave his coffee unattended on the nightstand before standing up to shake hands.

"This shit is hilarious," John says. "I wish we would have had the time to add audio to the feed as well."

Then it's so quick we almost miss it. While Benjamin is shaking hands with Xander, Pixie takes advantage of the interaction by reaching over and spiking the Trojan horse. I see her exhale clearly with satisfaction, then look up to the camera, giving us the thumbs up sign while crossing her eyes and smiling.

"YESSSSS!!!!!" We both say in unison.

Now we watch as it looks like Xander is explaining about the last X-rays needed before Clarissa can be released. He touches Clarissa's face tenderly, knowing how much it still hurts, and points out the damage that concerns him. Xander is an excellent actor, but John and I can see his sorrow shadow his eyes as he fights to stay in character for the good of a successful extraction. Benjamin seems to be listening, nodding his head in agreement, but never takes his eyes off Clarissa's face. Slowly, she looks over at him and returns a contemptible stare, boring years of loathsome hate directly into his eyes. We don't need sound or subtitles to figure out what's happening or what she's going to say. We can see clearly her determined show of defiance and watch her face harden when she uses all her pent-up rage to pull her hand away. He begins grabbing for the hand he just lost control of, not believing she would dare to act with such insolence. Score one for Clarissa, as she continues to slap at him and cries out with what we believe to be: "Don't touch me!!!!!"

All of us see the look on her face and hope she can continue to be that strong during the hours and days ahead. Xander leans over the bed, putting his hands out to try to diffuse the situation, as Pixie jumps in between the bed and Benjamin to protect her patient, pointing to the door and indicating for him to leave.

John stops his pacing and mutters, "Take it easy, Pix, he's unpredictable."

"I don't think she cares, John, look at her face! That's one pissed-off Pixie."

Benjamin backs up and lifts his hands in surrender, but before he turns, he grabs his cup of coffee from the nightstand and heads for the door but doesn't leave. Instead, he leans his shaking frame against the door, drinking coffee and seething because of the rebelliousness coming from his wife. After more than a few sips of the drug-laced coffee, he straightens. It looks like he's demanding to know how long it will take for the X-rays. He is visibly losing it with every second that ticks off in the corner of our feeds.

"It won't matter pretty soon, you bastard, because you're about to find yourself waking up into a nightmare you can't control," I hiss at my little screen.

We watch the feed as Pixie leaves the room, giving Benjamin a look of disdain as she exits. Xander continues to stand by Clarissa's bedside for support, secretly wishing Benjamin would make a move so he could knock him out before the drug does. Pixie returns moments later with a wheelchair and begins to help Clarissa into it. When she straightens up from positioning Clarissa's feet on the pedals, she looks up to the camera and gives a nod of her head toward the door. John and I see

Benjamin is having trouble standing, so we know it won't be long before he's down and out. Xander notices this also, and after Pixie wheels Clarissa out of the room, he steps over and retrieves the chair Benjamin had occupied earlier. He positions it tightly against the wall, close to the door, and aggressively pushes Benjamin into it. Benjamin doesn't make a move to resist as his head leans back against the wall and his arms swing from the sides of the chair. At this point, Xander decides to rewrite this scene, giving Dr. Thadius the chance to take center stage again and do some improv. So, with no warning to us watching this black-and-white soundless production, he strikes out with his right fist, connecting solidly with Benjamin's right cheek. Satisfied with his performance, he bows to the camera, giving us a salute. As Benjamin begins to slide out of the chair to connect with the floor, Dr. Thadius makes his dramatic exit, and the imaginary credits begin to roll.

"Damn, that was satisfying even without sound," John laughs. "Sleep tight, Benji."

"That was a pretty good right cross for a Doctor," I say, surprised.

"He wasn't always a Doctor!" John states evasively, closing off his laughter. Causing me to once again, wonder about Xander's story, adding more intrigue to the reason why he became a part of Mickey.

Chapter 18

"Here we go," John mutters when we hear a hurried knock on the door. He opens the door wide enough to allow the wheelchair to enter the room, then waits impatiently to close off the view into the room from any out-of-the-know eyes. "I've got The Dreadlock Kid watching your back tonight, Reg. He requested the detail knowing how bad this one could get. The Dreadlock Kid's real name is Oscar-D, and he wears his dreads proudly. After you left this morning, he entered your motel rooms and placed the mics to make sure all is up and running for when you get there. He's parked out back by your car in a white van displaying the logo of an out-of-town Electric Company. He'll follow you back to the motel and park a few rooms down. He'll be in constant contact with Matt, who will be on Benjamin every second after he wakes from his nap."

"Thank you, John," I say sincerely and mean it more than he will ever know.

Once Pixie has pushed the wheelchair through the door and secured the brakes, Clarissa looks around the room, spotting John and myself before reaching out to clasp Pixie's hand. "Thank you, thank you," she says, holding onto Pixie tightly, feeling safe for the first time in years. Then she lets go of Pixie's protection and looks at me. "So, these are your friends," she says, looking from me to John, then back up to Pixie. "Thank you, thank you all."

"Just a few of them," I answer with deep unease because now four of us have been compromised. At this point, Pixie takes over by pulling a pair of scrubs out of a drawer she had planted earlier, along with Clarissa's shoes she took from her personal belongings bag issued the night she was admitted. She asks John to step out for a few minutes so she can help Clarissa change. When Clarissa is dressed, I step over to the door and let John know the coast is clear. Noticing the goosebumps on Clarissa's arms, Pixie removes the sweater she's been wearing over her scrub top and helps Clarissa into it. With a quivering smile, Clarissa nods her thanks and is again overwhelmed with the woman's kindness, pulling the sweater tight around her middle.

"Thank you, Pix, that was well done," I hear John say. "Remember what comes next and be careful. I'll continue to watch the feed from here until Benjamin wakes up and leaves the hospital. At that point, Matt will be our eyes. As discussed, once he starts waking up, I'll alert you via text. I'm gearing up for a terrible scene when he does, so you should too."

"Got it, Boss," she replies. Standing next to Clarissa, she straightens, her body language showing she's trying to control her emotions. She reaches into her scrub top pocket, removing a small prescription bottle, and hands it to me. "This will get her through the night if she needs them." Then with watery eyes, she gives me a nod and says, "Please take care of our girl."

"I will, Pix, I promise."

"Thank you again, Pixie," Clarissa says. "Please do as he says," she indicates with a nod of her head toward John, "you need to be extremely careful. Especially after he reads my goodbye letter because he's going to blame you for my running. Benjamin is mean and can be so conniving and unpredictable," she blurts out with years of pent-up rage, perpetuated by the constant twists and turns of more than a decade of riding an emotional roller coaster. I wish I could say that the twists and turns will begin to straighten, but that's not the case. This emotional roller coaster is coming around the bend, leaving her tunnel of captivity to enter another tunnel of indecision and uncertainty. She still has a lot of unfamiliar track ahead, and we can only hope she doesn't get derailed with second thoughts.

"I'll be fine," Pixie says and leans down for a hug so strong it looks like she's scared to let go. "Fine, I'll be just fine," she says to Clarissa, trying to reassure her.

I witness the interaction, and it brings to mind all the questions we, as individuals, need to answer before becoming a member of Mickey. Internally, we've all studied multiple imaginary pages of self-assessment, the hope that we can recognize our weaknesses and feed our strengths. We've all read them numerous times, the multitude of meanings deciphered differently for each of us. The nonexistent pages yellowed with time, their highlighted passages screaming out to each of us from memory. We've devoured the words on each page earnestly, taken the imaginary quiz in the back multiple times. We refer back to them whenever we are second-guessing our resolve, whether it be from success or loss. Not everyone will make it, but it's up to each of us to determine if we'll continue to study. Some will push forward, learning to reel in their emotions like a retractable dog leash, and some will begin to realize their limits and retreat. Each time we revisit the pages, we hope to discover something new, something promising that will speak to each of us individually. We hope we will find a spark of knowledge pertaining to our personal stories that will revive us once again. It's a unique individual handbook carried by each of us. It delves into our private nuances in order to help develop a critically strong mental attitude needed for this job. But this interaction between Pixie and Clarissa shows me there is still work for Pixie to do. She still needs the imaginary pages and all the knowledge they can deliver. She needs to study them completely and accept them with honest clarity. She's obviously strong physically, but she's still letting her empathy override her ability to keep her distance emotionally. The stakes are too high for her to lose herself in the murky waters of human emotion, the dark water making it hard to separate the two. The dissection of emotion should never be perceived as black and white, murky, or clear; it's just not that easy. It means training your thoughts and emotions in order to maintain your distinct individualism. And it's obvious at this point that she needs to focus on her mental health, ask herself the hard questions, so her overall existence isn't placed in jeopardy.

Where I can construct barriers to keep from forming an attachment to the Rescued, or them to me, not everyone has that ability. That's because they've never been a victim as I have; they've never had to exist by emotionally shutting down. They've never had to close an emotional trap door of fear to gain just a few minutes of peace. Yes, they've all got a story, but they weren't "the" story. I hope she won't become an emotional train wreck because she became a member of our team, but unfortunately, I've seen it before. People get too involved, too emotionally attached, finding it harder and harder to take even the favorable outcomes as successes. They feel a deep loss and emptiness when a Rescue placed in their care moves into the next phase, leaving them behind to be turned over to another member of Mickey to complete the process. Through the years, we've all shown multiple tirades of emotion; we all react to the reasons for loss differently, no matter the aspect, good or bad. But in order to do this job successfully, we have to be able to balance compassion in one hand and control our emotions in the other. Because when we let sadness and doubt begin to weigh us down and become a burden, it's time to walk away, and that's okay. The harsh reality is, at the end of the day, we'll either make it, or we won't. I hope Pixie makes it because we need compassion like hers, but we need her mentally strong in order to succeed.

Chapter 19

John continues to watch the feed of Benjamin drooling all over himself while I walk Clarissa through the plan for getting her out of here. John keeps updating me on Benjamin's status. He tells me Benjamin is still knocked out cold, and I can tell he doesn't care if it's from the drug or the well-deserved punch to his face; it makes no difference to him. All his training in the military has taught him restraint just as much as honor, on and off the battlefield. Right now, his body's natural reaction to restraint is strong, but his heart is telling him to ignore his training because, in this situation, it's totally misguided. He feels shackled by the restraint but feels like rejoicing as its hold on him begins to skid to a halt toward this man who wouldn't know honor if it jumped up and bit him on the ass. So, sitting here, watching Benjamin sleep, he wonders how much longer he can hold back. He thinks of his Aunt Michelle and, as always, lets the guilt rush in on him. The thought of not being able to help her will forever eat away at his being. Feeling the regret as a raw invasion, he shakes his head and drops his eyes to the time stamp on his screen, calculating Benjamin has been asleep for about thirty minutes. He figures that gives them at least another hour and a half to make sure Clarissa is safely tucked in with Reggie watching over her, and Oscar-D watching over Reggie.

I help Clarissa up from the wheelchair, asking if she thinks she can go down two flights of stairs and out to my car. She says yes, but her demeanor and eyes seem hesitant. "We'll take it slow," I assure her. "We have some time, okay?" John holds the door open, telling me to be careful as we slip out. Clarissa and I whisper our goodbyes as we head down the hall. I look back one last time and see John watching us until we open the door to head down the stairs. I silently send him my thanks, as I have hundreds of times, for being one of my guardian angels.

After we have left, John watches Pixie enter the hospital room to check on Benjamin. He's still out cold on the floor in front of the chair where he fell from grace after hitting Xander's fist with his face. With his head leaning back into the seat of the chair and mouth wide open, it looks like he's snoring loudly into the room. John watches her and knows what she's thinking. At this point, every new member of Mickey gets caught up in it—the need to deliver just a semblance of the pain the abuser has dished out. He deserves to be a victim, to live day in and day out with no hope of freedom and smothered in constant fear. She can't help but be angry at the small dose of pain he received; to her, a punch in the face didn't even come close to payback. He got off easy, too easy as far as she's concerned. She bends over the pathetic bastard and looks closely at his face, where a bruise is already beginning to form. She wants so much to add another one; she's visibly trembling with that military engrained restraint. But instead, she stands and heads out of the room, dimming the lights before closing the door behind her. Now she waits for the confrontation she knows is coming and is so looking forward to it.

John decides to take the chair Reggie has vacated while he watches the seconds tick off in the corner of the feed. It has been almost three hours since Benjamin hit the floor, and he is now beginning to stir. John sends Pixie a quick text, "WAKING UP, GET IN THERE!!!"

Watching Benjamin fumble around trying to get to his feet is like a scene from *The Walking Dead*. He staggers around, bumping into the chair, knocking it over as he falls against the wall. Rubbing his eyes and shaking his head as if to clear it, he looks around the room, remembering where he is and who's missing. John watches Benjamin's entire body stiffen after he looks at the clock on the wall and begins to clench his jaw. His hand shoots up to rub his face, and the camera picks up the visible reaction to the pain, which satisfies, on a small scale, some of John's hatred. Benjamin abruptly heads for the door, but it begins to open before he can get his hand on the handle. Standing in the doorway is Benjamin's biggest obstacle in a very compact package. John watches and knows Pix can take care of herself but is also comforted by the fact that the security guard standing right outside the door is a member of Mickey also.

Pixie stands in the doorway like a mini linebacker, determined to cause Benjamin as much deserved pushback as she can. "Where's my damn wife, you little Bitch, how the hell long does it take for X-rays in this place?" Pix stands her ground; the only reaction she displays is to fold her arms around a hospital chart, hugging it close to her chest. Her look of contempt toward him is screaming into the camera. The camera picks up Benjamin's agitation, making John feel he's in the room and can hear Benjamin's voice begin to rise as he continues to scream his demands. "I want you to tell me where my wife is and RIGHT.THE.FUCK.NOW, and where's that screwy Dr.?" She still doesn't respond, sending him to new heights of anger even he hasn't felt before. "Why did I wake up on the floor with a splitting headache and my face feeling like I've been in a barroom brawl? Tell me what's going on; I need my wife!" he aggressively screams in Pix's face. John can literally see the spittle fly from Benjamin's mouth as his tirade continues. He advances toward her, but she reads his body language. Without him even seeing her movements, she reaches out with her foot and lifts the chair by one of its legs, throwing it in his direction, cutting off his path to her. "I want my damn wife, AND RIGHT GOD DAMN NOW!!!!!" His strangled scream is directed at Pixie as he fights with the chair, cutting off his path to advance menacingly forward.

"She signed herself out; she left you," Pix says, waving the hospital chart out in front of him.

"What the hell are you talking about? Clarissa doesn't have the guts to make a move without me telling her to. I control every move she makes. So, you better tell me where she is, or 'you' are going to regret it. WHERE IS MY WIFE, DAMN IT!!!" He advances on her again, the hindrance of the chair forgotten. He begins assaulting the air with a fist directed at her face. But the blow never had a chance to connect as Pix deflects it with a quick swipe of the hard plastic hospital chart.

"Like I said," she advances on him with a murderous look, "she signed herself out. Here's the discharge form she signed; that is her signature, isn't it?" Pix knew it was Clarissa's signature; she watched her sign it earlier that morning when they were discussing how things were going to play out. Internally, she wanted to use some of her combat training to lay this bastard out but reeled in her thoughts, knowing his day would come soon enough.

Benjamin looks at the chart, breathing heavily, boring holes into the hard plastic clipboard the paper is secured to. He has no words to spit through his escalating anger, not believing Clarissa would have found the determination and courage to defy him, to disrespect him. He rears his right arm back and slams his fist into the wall next to Pixie's head.

Her eyes deliberately twinkle at him, showing she's not afraid and can't be intimidated. He can't control her like he did Clarissa, and now he can't even control Clarissa. Calming a bit, he raises his fist to his chest and massages his knuckles. "Where's my wife?" Pix notices his tone has changed, his eyes growing darker than they were five minutes earlier. A sudden fear grips her like nothing she has ever experienced, even in Iraq. She sends a quick look up to the camera, knowing John is there to have her back is enough to help her maintain her strength. She continues to stand defiantly in the doorway, showing him she's okay, she has this.

"I don't know!" she spits back the truth into the space between them. For everyone's protection, she really had no idea where Clarissa was taken, "But she wanted me to give you this." Pixie reaches into her pocket and removes the letter Clarissa had given her earlier. He just stares at the paper, again not believing this could really be happening. He is filled with a dark rage only he can feel, the same rage Clarissa took the brunt of hundreds of times over the years. Pixie loves his disbelief, relishing his confusion, but continues to hold out the letter. Even though she's shaking internally, she doesn't drop her hand, half expecting smoke to come pouring out of his ears and little red horns to pop out of his head. He finally tears it from her hand and skims the words, shaking his head as his body trembles with agitated fury, its turmoil just waiting to erupt.

"She wouldn't do this on her own; you made her write this. You and that stupid Doctor. I'm calling the police!"

"I wouldn't do that if I were you," she says, showing him the other documents included in Clarissa's medical chart. They were copies of all the previous Emergency Room visits, all the X-rays, all the Doctor's notes that treated her in each instance, and plenty more questionable documents screaming abuse. "Besides, she's an adult who signed herself out, and you said this is her signature," Pix reminds him while pointing to the discharge papers again. "There's nothing the police can do for you. I really don't know where she is, but I know it's not under your thumb anymore, Benjamin." John is uneasy with how Benjamin's temper is escalating and nervous for Pix, but proud of her backbone. He watches Benjamin charge toward the door, pushing Pixie out of the way as he passes her. Pixie looks up and nods into the camera, then leaves the room as well. On that note, the first phase of the extraction is complete, and John sends a quick text to Matt: "HE'S ON THE MOVE!" Matt responds with: "ON IT, BOSS!"

Chapter 20

Once Clarissa and I are in the stairwell, we make it down the two flights of stairs and head to the door leading out of the hospital. We push through the door, and I immediately start scanning the parking lot. It's an engrained response for safety before making a dash toward Oscar-D and the white van he's waiting in. The van is parked right next to my car, and I see Suzie looking through the window into the van. I don't even need to get any closer because I know she's whining her concerns to the driver. Oscar-D has moved to the passenger seat of the van with the window down, speaking softly to her, trying to lower the level of anxiety crashing down inside the confines of my car. "It's okay, girl; she'll be fine and back soon with a new friend for you to watch over," Oscar-D whispers.

I hustle Clarissa to the Explorer and tell her to get in the back seat, stay low, and cover up with the blanket I keep there. She heads that way, causing Suzie to hit new heights of maternal frenzy because she's been waiting for me and her new charge for what seems like hours. After a few words with Oscar-D, I open my door and jump in, where I'm immediately attacked with furry concern and a wet, half-naked, headless baby. "Oh, Suzie," I say, "I'm sorry I was gone so long, but you shouldn't have taken your concerns out on your baby." I give her a well-deserved hug as I look into the back seat to make sure Clarissa had followed my instructions. When I quickly see that she has, I'm instantly horrified with all the dog hair clinging to the blanket and feel terrible. I can only hope she likes dogs. Turning the key, I give a quick nod to the left at Oscar-D before heading away from the hospital and what I hope is Clarissa's past.

"How ya doin' back there, you still with me?" I ask, taking a glance into the back seat and seeing Clarissa poke her head out from under the blanket. She doesn't say anything, just nods her head up and down, and I can see even with a quick glance, how scared she is. "Good, we're almost there, and we'll get you settled. Just hold on a bit longer," I tell her.

I glance into my side mirror and am relieved to see Oscar-D's van a couple of cars behind me. But even though I know he's there, I've learned that this is where unexpected surprises can pop up. I'm pretty confident this won't be the case because I know Benjamin was still out cold when we left. Suzie leans into my right shoulder, giving me support and comfort because her motherly instinct knows it's what I need. "I'll find you a new baby as soon as we get back," I say, not taking my eyes off the road in front of me. She licks my cheek in understanding, as if to say, "Don't worry about me right now; we have work to do."

My pulse is on overdrive, my heart beating with an intense rhythm I hope my rib cage can contain. My knuckles are white on the steering wheel, and my hands feel as cold as ice, the reaction all too normal to me in these situations. I lift my foot off the gas as we come to a stop sign. I slowly let out a breath and lift my cramped fingers from their vice-like grip on the wheel once we've stopped. We are two blocks from the motel, and I can't wait to get behind the safety of our room door. Oscar-D is now one car behind me, and as our procedures indicate, he will go through the stop sign and make a couple of passes around the block. When he is satisfied we are clear, he'll pull into the motel and head to the back. He knows I will have already hustled Clarissa into our connecting rooms, so he will park a few rooms down and begin his security tour. Or as I like to call it, his guarding of my personal galaxy. I wasn't surprised when John told me he had volunteered for this detail. He is young and high-strung at times but possesses a strong passion to keep me safe and help victims. He's funny in a cocky sort of way; the eagerness of youth is out of control sometimes but for all the right reasons. I figured out over the years what his story is: it's that he has no story. He just knows we need his help, so he comes running. Over time, we've learned he does much better mentally if he is on surveillance and guardian details consisting only of himself rather than with a partner. Apparently, no one gets his humor but me, and it bugs the shit out of his partners. I've had many Guardians over the years besides Oscar-D and am so unbelievably grateful to each and every one. They've had to pull my ass out of sticky situations too many times for me not to be.

It's now 1:30 pm, and I am unlocking the door to our adjoining rooms. I quickly push the door open and head in with Suzie and Clarissa on my heels. We stand in the silence, adrenaline pushing our lungs to the max, inhaling and exhaling high levels of air carried by altered breaths. With invisible mouthfuls of air, our spent lungs slowly begin to retract their breaths, holding them in for a few sweet seconds before sending them back out into the soft rays of light gleaming through the curtains.

I don't say a word as I take a quick peek through the opening in the curtain, looking for the van with my Guardian inside. He sees me and sends me a text that all is good. I'm instantly relieved and respond with a capital "THANK YOU." He sends me another text asking if we're hungry. I look over at Clarissa and think that's a good idea. It will calm us down some, I think, as we begin to get to know each other. I will begin to explain the near future and what she can expect from us and what we will demand from her. I respond with "YES, JUST SURPRISE US ☺☺, THANK YOU!"

I turn and slowly walk toward Clarissa, who is standing next to the bed. I can clearly see she is scared and uncertain. "Please sit for a bit; you're safe now." I walk over to the connecting door of our rooms and open it wide, "The only rule I have is this door stays open at all times." She shakes her head with exaggerated understanding, pulling the sweater tighter around her middle.

"Thank you, Reggie. I don't know what else to say. You have helped me where I couldn't help myself. If not for you, I would have gone home with Benjamin and continued on in that hell." A single tear runs down her cheek, unhindered now by gauze but illuminated by multicolored bruises. The bandages came off this morning, but the fifteen stitches at her hairline are still there, and I ask her if she's seen her face. "No, I really didn't think or care about a mirror with everything else going on. Is it bad?"

"Yes and no. It's bad right now, but the only scar you will have externally is the one at your hairline, but your hair will hide it, so it won't be obvious at all. Do you want to look?" I ask hesitantly while walking slowly to the bathroom and turning on the light. I hear the soft movement of the bed as she stands up and walks toward me. Her face says, "This is nothing new for me; I've seen it all before," and that look saddens me deeply. I let her enter the bathroom as I step aside, giving her room. I watch the emotions sailing across her face and instantly feel like an intruder, so I reach for the door and close it, giving her some privacy and a chance to unburden her soul. I hear it immediately—the hard-wracking sobs that started in the pit of her stomach, fighting for purchase as they claw their way up her throat, burning with sorrow to be the first to escape. The sobs keep coming and coming, each one slicing through the anger in their need to escape and be free of the darkness that has held them prisoner. I watch Suzie pad her way to the door and lean her head close, listening to the torture as it bursts into the small space, wishing with all her might she could help.

"She's really broken, Suz, but we can help her if she lets us."

Chapter 21

Suzie and I continue to stand outside the bathroom door. The horror being released amplifies as it continues. The torrential onslaught of jagged screams is accompanied by the cleansing of tears that flow with the release of years of pent-up rage. Finally, I hear the water from the faucet splash into the basin, where I assume Clarissa is tenderly washing her face of residual tears. The blowing of her nose and flushing of the toilet give me a clue that she is spent and will be coming out soon. Another few minutes and she cracks the door open. Suzie is sitting eagerly at my feet, wanting to give Clarissa some mothering. She waits anxiously and looks at me, pleading for permission to do just that. I clear my throat and ask, "Do you like dogs?" Clarissa smiles hesitantly, looking down at Suzie before reaching out her hand to touch the damaged ear that holds a story of its own. "It's okay, Suz, she needs you now." With that, Suzie pushes herself in close to Clarissa, leaning into her body to surround it with all her understanding and love. Clarissa accepts the gesture as it was intended. Leaning down, she circles her arms around Suzie's neck to give her a slight squeeze.

"Thank you, Suzie. I needed that and you, right now." We hear my phone ping with a text, and I retrieve it off the table located under the window.

"Looks like our lunch will be here in a second, hope you're hungry." Just then there is a slight tap at the door, and I go to open it, but not until I look out the window to make sure it's the runner from the Club House. It's Dan, and he smiles at me through the window, waiting for me to open the door. He hands me two bags of delicious-smelling Italian food with a smile and a bow before turning to leave. "Thanks, Dan, did you make this yourself?" I ask, because Dan has been known to monopolize the kitchen in the Club House and turn out the most amazing food.

"Sorry to disappoint, Reg, didn't have enough time. I picked this up at the Italian place next to the airport on my way. I hope it's as good as mine. Wait, no, I don't," he says, laughing at me. He turns his eyes to Clarissa and nods his head, "Ma'am, you're in good hands now," then turns and closes the door behind him.

Clarissa and I sit at the table and try to eat. The food is excellent, but neither one of us can do justice to the portions on our plates. "How are you feeling? Do you need some pain meds or maybe a good nap?" She is drained from the days in the hospital, where sleep came only if pushed by medication but was evasive and intermittent when the doses were gradually cut back. I can see she is tired, so I suggest the nap again. This time she agrees to go lie down for a bit. "We'll talk after you're rested," I say and walk her into the other room. "Clarissa, you're safe with us," I say after she is settled on the bed. I wanted her to hear that before she tried to sleep; maybe it will help her to drift off and actually get some rest. I place the bottle of meds next to her on the nightstand, but she declines the offer, hoping sleep will come on its own.

Suzie and I snuggle up on our bed. Her new baby, with its head still attached, is cradled within her paws of protection. I know napping isn't an option for me as there is still too much to figure out. First of all, I have to find a way to tell Clarissa about her mother, but I can't entertain the thought of piling the sad news onto her shoulders just yet. She has no idea what emotional turmoil is waiting for her tonight, and she doesn't need another level of reality betraying her resolve to fight. The veracity of her actions hasn't hit her yet. The decisions she will have to make to move forward still seem unclear, but all of it will come slamming down soon enough. The terror of actually facing what she has done, the what-ifs, and the what's-next scenarios are going to be terrifying, but so far she seems to be handling everything as well as can be expected. She just escaped the iron bars of her cage of confinement, still not knowing if the door will swing shut and stay permanently closed behind her.

Suzie's head pops up when she hears the soft whimper coming from the other room. I lay my hand across her back to keep her with me. I know all she wants to do is go to Clarissa and comfort her through her dream, the first of many that will emerge from the lingering of her past. "Stay now, Suz. If it gets too bad, we'll go in and comfort her, okay? You are such a good girl; how does your heart not break with all the concern you carry inside." We hear the scream escape from the bed, and both of us jump up and run into the adjoining room. Suzie jumps onto the bed to protect Clarissa as I start to speak softly to her and hold her hand. I don't want to scare her any more than she already is.

"NO, NO, not again, I thought it was what you wanted. I didn't do anything wrong. Please don't, don't!!!" She begins to crawl out of the darkness of her past, screaming in my face, thinking I'm Benjamin. I try to grab her arms to stop the onslaught of thrashing around, but she continues to push me away, trying to escape the pain that would have normally come. As I'm doing my best to calm her down, Suzie manages to lie across her middle to keep her from hurting herself—and me.

"Clarissa, Clarissa, it's me, Reggie. Please calm down before you hurt yourself." I can feel the dream fading from her body, the darkness clearing to a heavy gray as she pushes her way out of her past. She's close to breaking through because she's starting to tremble in silence. I've been there, done that, still do that! When her eyes finally open and she realizes who I am and remembers where she is, she slumps with grateful relief.

"I'm sorry, I'm sorry!" she says in a hurried explanation, breathing rapidly to gulp in air. Suzie whines her understanding and places her baby in Clarissa's lap, her way of trying to calm her. She leans up and licks the tears from Clarissa's face, then picks up her baby again, encouraging her to accept it. "Thank you, Suzie," she says while looking at the soft bunny and holding it close. She continues to shake while she strokes Suzie behind the ear and says darkly, "I had a cat once. It was a stray that wandered onto our back porch, so I started feeding it. I would sit in a lawn chair and hold it to my chest and lose myself in its soft purr, needing the warm closeness. But Benjamin didn't like the idea of me loving it so much, so he took 'care' of it. He was even jealous of a cat!"

I sit down at the foot of the bed, willing to just listen if she wanted to share some more, but all she did was pet Suzie and look at the stuffed animal in her hand. Softly I begin, "You know, Clarissa, right now you are unbelievably broken, but with our help, you can begin to heal. I hope you can believe that. There is going to be an enormous number of doors of pain for you to close; some will stay closed and locked, some will just stay closed, and unfortunately, some will crack themselves open again from time to time. It's going to be a long road, but you will always have help. There are numerous levels of broken, Clarissa, but also unlimited levels of healing. There is so much out there just waiting for you. Your journey is just beginning, and eventually you'll walk in sunshine again."

I stand now and walk to the window, mostly out of habit than anything else. I look out and see Oscar-D watching over us diligently, delivering a sense of comfort. "Clarissa, this is where you need to recognize the possibility of a new life. You will mourn the loss of yourself and the life you had before Benjamin; that's only natural. The unnatural part will be finding the strength to work hard, and eventually forgive yourself for what you let him take from you... No, steal from you. You need to envision the life you can make on your own and leave him behind. This is your reality right now: either you move forward knowing it's going to be a struggle, or you head back to the life waiting in the darkness. You have a lot of thinking to do tonight, but I want you to know that no matter what you decide to do—stay or go—it's your choice." I move back to the bed, hoping common sense will prevail, but sometimes broken doesn't begin to describe the devastation floating around inside a lost soul. But the puzzle of her past, before Benjamin, needs to be put back together one piece at a time. Once she believes she can do it, the pieces will slowly fit together to form the intricate person she was before. Then slowly, she can begin to fit together the pieces of the new puzzle, where their interlocking strength will form the foundation for the person she will become.

She looks at me and nods her head. "I understand, I think." She molds Suzie's baby in her hands, petting it like it's the cat she once had. "Are you saying I can go back to Benjamin if I want to?" I nod yes. "Does that really happen? I mean, do the women you help actually go back?"

"It's happened a few times. The fear was just too strong and pulled them back. We lost a couple of women because they didn't think that it could get any worse than it was before they left. But they learned soon enough: it can always get worse."

The tears come now, and she looks at me. "I've been trying to figure out how this happened to me. How I allowed him to totally consume every part of my life, every part of me." With so much shame emanating off her bruised face, she begins a crying jag that consumes her whole body with sobs of pain. "He wasn't like this when we met," she says, wiping tears from her face. "I can't figure out what I did wrong."

"Yes, he was!!! And you did nothing wrong!"

"He always says he's sorry!"

"He's not!"

"He says he loves me!"

"He can't!"

"He always says it won't happen again!"

"It will; you know it will! Clarissa, you did nothing wrong. Please don't allow him to linger in your head and manipulate you into making a bad decision. We both know he's not here physically, but he's in here," I say, tapping my temple. "This is where you begin to heal. This first decision is the hardest, but it's also the beginning."

She opens her mouth to answer but changes her mind, leaving only silence to mingle among us. Ironically, all abusers follow the same pattern: they're always sorry, it'll never happen again, they always claim to love you. Hell, who knows, maybe they actually believe the sick bullshit they spew. But I know what they really are. They're hunters, sadistic chameleons on two legs, changing their personalities instead of colors to ensnare their prey. They sneak into the hopes and dreams of their chosen one, luring them in behind a camouflage of fake emotion and smiles. They are experts at the game, hiding their real selves and sick desires behind the persona they allow you to see.

"Like I said, you have a lot of thinking to do tonight. But there is something I need to tell you before I leave you to it. We were able to find your mother. She's still alive but extremely ill."

"What? Where is she? What do you mean, ill? How bad?" She is kneeling on the bed now, facing me with a heightened sadness rushing over her face, trying to get the questions answered as quickly as they're asked. I relay the information Abby gave us as best I can, hoping I didn't leave anything out. I watch the news sink in as Clarissa changes position on the bed, trying to take it all in.

"I'm so sorry, Clarissa, but I want you to know that she has Guardians watching her around the clock to protect her from Benjamin. So keep that in mind when you're making your decision."

"Oh no, oh God, I have to go back now. That's the first place he'll go; I need to go back." She begins to get up from the bed, but I catch her arm gently.

"I told you we're watching him and your mother, and we will continue watching until we know he's not a threat. I promise you!"

She's trying to pull away from me to head for the door, but I step in front of her, blocking her movements. "You don't understand!" she screams, "He'll go there looking for me, and if he doesn't find me, he'll make good on his threat and take his rage out on her." Tears are soaking into her top as they flow with emotional pain. She continues to try and pull her arm away from me, but I stand firm in front of her.

"Clarissa, listen to me," I say, leaning in just inches from her face. I'm holding both her arms now, forcing her eyes to seek mine. "If you go back now, he might not go after your mom right away, but he may later just to teach you a lesson. But putting all that aside, do you seriously think he will welcome you back with open, forgiving arms?"

"Of course he won't welcome me back with open arms! If I'm lucky, he'll just beat the living crap out of me instead of kill me!" Her voice is rising to a level of pure panic as she spits the words of unwavering certainty in my face. "But I'd rather he took his rage out on me than on an innocent, frail woman. Oh God, how did this happen? How did I let this happen?" She sags to the floor, pulling me with her, and we end up on our knees facing each other. She tips her head back against the emotional pain and lets loose high-pitched cries and screams like that of an animal claiming its place in the wild. Her screeches of sorrow encourage the horrific memories of him to slip in, dark and silent, moving covertly to remind her of what he can do. They're adding to her pain like a sharp knife delivering its intrusion of terror, thrust after thrust directly into her being. The weapon shines with purchase through her fear. With each stab and sickening twist, it looks for the right time to pounce on any inclination of defiance. She experiences a primal fear like she's the prey, and Benjamin is the demonic hunter of her soul, leaving her hurting like a wounded animal. Through the racking sobs, she screams, "I want to see for myself that she's safe! I need to see her even if she doesn't remember me!"

"I'm telling you, I promise you, she's protected. If you stay with us, we will make sure you get to see her; we'll make sure you get to her in time." Suzie begins to move her soft body in between us, leaning from one to the other as she tries to calm each of us individually with what she knows we need. Clarissa is physically absorbing everything she heard. I can see each word I said play across her face as she dissects it for flaws and lies. I'm hopeful as I see she's at least listening, hopeful that what I've said will contribute to her making the right decision, what "I" think is the right decision. I drop my hands to my knees before standing, wishing I had some magic trick to pull from a hat or could wave a wand to help her see the light, but I don't. I stand up, dropping my hands to my sides and exhale my resolve with a nod, feeling I've done all I can. The rest is up to her now. "The door is unlocked and there's the phone," I say, indicating with the wave of my hand. "Suzie and I will be in our room if you need anything."

Suzie follows me to the door, leaving her baby with Clarissa, knowing she needs it right now for comfort. Before I walk through the adjoining door, I stop, wanting to make sure what I am about to say registers with her. I turn back to the room, crossing my arms across my chest, leaning my shoulder into the doorjamb, and face her. "Clarissa, until you can look me in the eye and tell me you're ready to do whatever it takes to move forward, I can't, I won't invest my team any further or put them in danger. I won't allow you to keep us from investing our resources in someone who will look me in the eye and vow to give it their all. You see, Clarissa, the members of my team have insurmountable reserves of compassion and heartfelt desire to help anyone they can, but I won't subject them to an emotional, unnecessary failure if I see it's a possibility. What we're offering you is a chance to run from a horrific past and chase a bright future. We're offering you a chance to leave all the heartache behind, and we'll do that by helping you fight the demons of your past. But know this, there's a big difference—no, huge difference—between surviving and being a survivor. That's what we're offering you, the opportunity to find the old you and then build the new you. It won't be easy by any means; you'll gain ground and then lose it. You'll feel empowered, then be slapped down with the harsh reality of your past. It's going to take all the strength you think you lost, all the fight you gave away and more—much more—before you'll be able to say, 'I'm a survivor.'" I wait for a response as she stands beside the bed, but the soft glow of the lamp light being snuffed out abruptly is what I get. I hope that action indicates my words were absorbed as I intended because that's all I can wish for. "I'm taking Suzie out for her walk, remember you're safe here." No response from the dark room.

Before I take Suzie out for her walk, I pop what is left of my lunch into the small microwave and heat it up for Oscar-D. I feel bad he isn't going to get dinner tonight. I open the door and step outside, giving him a nod as we pass the van and head to Suzie's personal spot to do her business. When she's done, we make our way back to the van, where we will sit and wait. After I'm seated and Suzie is comfortable, I hand the food over to Oscar-D, who lavishes me with thanks and digs in. I'm once again drawn in, watching this young man who never wavers from an assignment or duty of any kind—a what-you-see-is-what-you-get kind of guy. He's tall, stocky, and sports some amazing dreadlocks whose ends change color at least once a week. Yellow today, yuck!

"So, what do you think, Miss Reggie? Are we wasting our time?" he asks with a mouthful of food.

"I'm not sure yet. Let's give her some time," I say with a sigh. "She knows everything now, so the ball's in her court. But if she goes back, it won't end well, I'm sure of that much." We listen in on the sobbing emanating through the small mics Oscar-

D planted earlier when I was at the hospital. The pain of doubt, mistrust, and the unknown is pushed through the devices, finding their way into the van, demonstrating our most invasive action. It's so hard to just sit and raid a person's personal horror, but we need to be ready if her decision is to leave. So, we continue to listen through the crying, waiting for the two-sided coin of indecision to drop and roll to a stop, showing her and us the way.

"Just heard from Matt," Oscar-D says through another mouthful of food. "Benjamin is freaking out like some feral beast. His words, not mine," he says, washing down his last bite with a swallow of Red Bull. "He hasn't left the hospital parking lot since he woke up and exited the building. Matt says he's escalating but can't figure out what Benjamin's next move will be."

"Whatever it is, it won't be good. He's the most sinister individual I've seen in a long time."

We notice the crying has stopped, and I hope Clarissa has managed to fall asleep. But just then we see the door of her room open, the light from the room casting a soft glow through the opening, surrounding her and the fear she wears so tightly. "Reggie, Suzie, are you out there?" she whispers as loud as she dares. The mics in the room are still able to pick up her whispered plea, but just barely. Suzie looks through the windshield and gives an agitated whimper, her eyes flying between Oscar-D and myself. Clarissa calls to us again and waits, but when she doesn't get a response, she slowly closes the door.

We hear the receiver of the phone being picked up, and our stomachs clench with dreaded anticipation. Neither of us speaks, we just wait for the pain of failure to overwhelm us. But there is no sound to indicate she is dialing a number. As the dial tone begins to scream with impatience through the wires, waiting to be prompted, my lungs have stopped pulling in air. I can't blink; my undamaged eyelid is stuck wide open, and I can't control my nerves as they begin their electrifying dance of dread through my whole body. Then suddenly, we hear the click of the receiver being placed back in its cradle, shutting down the incessant call of the dial tone. The muffled sounds now are of sniffing and nose blowing. Once more, she begins to cry, the mic picking up the clear determination laced with sorrow. She cries for the years she has lost with her mother. She whimpers in pain for all the individualism she allowed to be taken from her, all the individual actions and thoughts she was forbidden. She thinks her cowardice proves she deserved what she let happen and what she allowed to be taken from her. She continues to weep for losing herself to him and hopes it's not too late for her to remember who she was. The cries are once again funneled through unused defiance, followed with pent-up rage. It's clear to both of us as we sit and listen: she's reclaiming a small amount of the lost strength she let be taken. We both acknowledge what we are hearing at the same time. We not only know what her decision is but can hear it in her sobs as they find their way into the van.

"Well, that was excruciating on so many levels," I say and turn to Oscar-D and Suzie. "Looks like we have work to do."

"Yep, good job, Miss Reggie," Oscar-D says and wipes his mouth with a napkin. "Ummm, what you said about protecting your team, that's the sign of a good leader. Sadly, there are all kinds of battlefields we need to muck through, emotional and physical." With that being said, he reaches out to scratch Suzie's ear with affection. "Just wanted you to know your determination to protect your team is appreciated."

As usual, I don't know how to respond, so I don't. "I better get back in there," I say, opening the door. I look over my left shoulder and clear my throat as emotion threatens to escape. "We don't want to lose her now." Suzie concurs with my assessment by sniffing her response, giving Oscar-D a kiss before we leave the van.

"Wow, am I giving the Boss a run for his money with this girl, or what!"

"Don't count on it," I say as my feet hit the gravel next to the van. "Speaking of the Boss, will you fill him in on the situation? I'm sure he's got his hands full with tracking Benjamin's actions. Oh, and I wouldn't let him know you think you're giving him a run for his best girl's heart. You just might find yourself out of work." I laugh and start to close the door but stop. Looking up at the young man, I say, "Oscar-D, your words are appreciated also." I close the door behind me and head to the room, feeling strange but thinking to myself, family, a precious gift...

I slowly open the door to mine and Suzie's room and immediately see Clarissa sitting at the foot of my bed with her legs crossed under her. She looks at me through tear-soaked lashes, the eyes behind the wet curtains saying, *I'm looking you in the eye, and I'm done being a doormat.* "Reggie," she says, "I'm broken, like you said, so broken, but I don't want to be. I'm ready to do whatever you tell me to. I need to see my mother, and I'll fight as hard as I can to find a life of my own. Please help me!"

Chapter 23

We talk well into the night. Questions are asked and answered, assurances are given, and rivers of tears flow. And through it all, smiles manage to emerge momentarily here and there, depicting a sorrowful exhaustion from both of us. With everything we exchange this night, I grow convinced she is ready to trust us and move forward. Clarissa will learn soon enough we will always be here to help her through an active struggle of war between two worlds—her past and her future. And at times, it will seem never-ending, but ultimately it will be up to her to conquer her own demons and shut Benjamin down. I explain to her that tomorrow I will be taking her to our headquarters, where we will be staying for a while. There she will be able to heal and become strong enough to begin her journey. Like all her unrelated sisters before her, she shows emotions of surprise, doubt, hope, and an entire gamut of others. But most of all, she is enormously grateful to the organization and what we are offering her. Her main concern is still her mother. She wants to be with her as soon as possible. I have some ideas concerning this request and will discuss them with Abby as soon as possible. But for now, we need to catch a little sleep in order to function clearly tomorrow.

I send a quick text to my Guardian, letting him know we are going to try to get some sleep before morning appears. He responds, *SWEET DREAMS ZZZZZZZZ*. I watch Clarissa leave my room and am relieved she has agreed to let us help her. It was touch and go there for a while. I head to my bed and notice Suzie isn't stuck to my hip as usual. She's sitting just outside the adjoining door to Clarissa's room as if she's waiting for something. It is obvious from her face she's experiencing a dilemma and isn't too happy with the fact I haven't noticed. "Oh crap, I'm sorry, Suz, I'll ask. Ummm, Clarissa, Suzie wants to know if you're done with her baby. She really wants to go to bed too," I say and wait for the response from the other room.

Her reply isn't immediate. It takes its time to fumble through the draining sorrow she has had to face emotionally as well as physically. The last few days have hit new heights of pain, but she's now realizing that she may be able to leave it behind.

She responds in a way that can be felt through the room, through the air between us, its emotional gratitude invisible to the naked eye but seen by understanding. It's obvious by the way her voice cracks that she's crying when she speaks to Suzie, but these tears are flowing with hope and the realization that she may make it through this hell. Her voice escapes the dark room but isn't dark itself as she calls to Suzie. "Come here, Suzie, she's waiting for you, sweet girl." I motioned for her to go get her baby, and she shoots up and off like a flash, landing on Clarissa's bed in a state of maternal turmoil to retrieve the stuffed animal. "Thank you so much for letting me hold her for a while. You are such a good momma," she says through tears of gratitude. Suzie doesn't wait around for any more compliments, her way of saying, *hold the gratitude because she's done sharing at this point*. She feels it was a job well done by all, but her canine ability for nurturing was slipping for everyone but her baby—and me, of course. Like the rest of us, she's also mentally and physically exhausted. "Good night, Reggie," I hear from the darkness of the adjoining room.

"Good night, Clarissa. Oh my God, what are we, the Waltons," I whisper as I fall into bed, thinking I just might be smiling.

The next morning, we are in the van with Oscar-D, entering the Club House through the motor pool as our procedures insist upon. After every protection detail is completed, the mechanics and techs go over the rig with a fine-tooth comb. A couple of team members will retrieve my car from the motel and deliver it to the motor pool for the same sweeping by the techs. For now, I will get Clarissa and myself settled into the Bunk House and show her around. She will meet with Xander in a bit to be examined and discuss what his plan is for her recovery while she's with us. Oscar-D is dragging ass behind us as we enter the Club House and are surrounded by all the morning activity. "Thank you, Oscar-D," I say. He just waves me off like that wasn't necessary, or he's just too exhausted to make a response as he heads to the Bunk House before us.

I stop and welcome Clarissa in, pointing to the facility with proud satisfaction. "This is where we will stay while you heal and figure out what it is you want to do next. Don't worry," I say hurriedly after

I see the panic in her eyes, "we'll help you." She gives her head a nod, happy to be reassured.

"I feel like Dorothy and I've just walked into a techno version of Oz," she says, turning in a circle to take it all in. "This is amazing. Do all these people work for you?"

"Not me alone. There are four of us who put this operation together. Well, five if you include Suzie, who by now has visited a number of desks to be lavished with affection and a treat, of course."

"I can't believe this!" Clarissa says with pure astonishment.

"Come on, let's get you settled," I say and head to the Bunk House as well. "We've got clean clothes for you in your room; I think the sizes are good. Pixie gave suggestions by looking at the stuff she saw from the night you were admitted to the hospital, plus all the toiletries you will need. I bet a hot shower sounds good right about now since we didn't take the time before we left the motel." We enter the bedroom where she will be staying and see all the items I just mentioned on the bed. "If there is anything else you want or need, just ask."

"Reggie," she whispers. "Do you think it will really work out for me?"

I step close to her side and gently turn her to face me. "If you want it to, it will, but not without determination and hard work. You need to dig down deep in your soul and acknowledge all the years of pain Benjamin has caused you," I say, pointing to her heart. "You need to feed off of it, let it wash over you like the acid it is. Let its acrid darkness fill your body with determination and raw tenacity because that's how you'll find your power. It will help you to find your resolve and the strength to fight against your past. We can help you achieve a future without physical and mental abuse, but our efforts won't mean anything if you don't step up. There will always be triggers from the past, Clarissa; it may be a smell, a voice, the way someone speaks to you, or even a song that will tempt you to crumble. I wish I could tell you this won't happen, but this is the price we pay for doing time in hell. These are the consequences of our reality from someone else's actions. This team," I say and point to the Club House, "consists of extraordinary people. Our security is made up of ex-military, and our medical staff is the finest in the country. We have a financial entity with a money wizard whose golden fingers make our money grow to bankroll our efforts. We have sympathetic people in all walks of life, in every city and town we can call upon if needed. No matter where you choose to go or what you decide to do, we have someone there to watch over you and help you achieve your goal. You can go to school, get a job, or pick up where you left off with life and plans you had for your future. You can do anything you want. It is going to be unbelievably difficult, but with our help, you can chase a new reality and leave the old one behind to begin again. Like I said before, we're incredibly good at what we do. But right now, the only thing I want you to do is get comfortable. And the only thing I want you to think about is a new name. Sound good? Also, you might want to think about getting some rest since we didn't get much last night."

"Yes, I can do that. I really want to get in the shower and put some clean clothes on first, though," she says with a smile. "Thanks again, Reggie."

"You deserve to be happy, Clarissa," I say while heading to the door.

Before I go find John and get a status update on Benjamin, I find my favorite bunk and place mine and Suzie's belongings next to it. My body is screaming for rest also, but it will have to wait; I need to know how the surveillance is going.

Chapter 24

I step out of the Bunk House entrance and immediately see John coming my way. "We're meeting in the conference room for a status report on Benjamin. We need you to join us," John says with a look that tells me it wasn't a request.

"Okay, just let me grab a cup of coffee first. Suzie," I call out, and she comes running. "Go with John to the conference room, girl," I say and point in its direction before continuing my quest for coffee. After retrieving my jolt of caffeine, I approach the glass walls of the conference room. I can see Marco and Matt have joined John, so with coffee in hand, I enter and take a seat next to John and wait, looking from one face to the other. Matt looks so tired his eyelids are drooping like the shades of a window pulled down halfway to block out the sun. He tries to shake off the tiredness swathing him tightly by running his hands over his stubbled face and through his thick black hair. The action did nothing to push him past his fatigue, so he drops his hands down to the table, accepting defeat, and lets out an exhausting yawn. He wears the shadow of exhaustion as a cloak, looking at us with the sleepless night he can't shake from his bloodshot eyes. He is the first one to speak by laying out the events of last night's surveillance, which began the minute Benjamin exited the hospital.

"We've watched many abusers deal with the fact they've lost control over their victim, but this guy is freakin' mental. He didn't even leave the parking lot all night; he just paced outside the entrance, like he was waiting for someone, or possibly trying to gain the courage to go back inside and raise hell. Or maybe he thinks Clarissa is still in there being hidden from him; I just don't know," he says, shaking his head. "At this point, I have no idea what to expect from this guy, except he's escalating and getting ready to explode. I gave Dominic my assessment when he took over this morning; he's as much in the dark as I am. He said he would keep us posted per usual protocols through the day. Sorry, Boss," he says, looking at John. "This guy is a hybrid version of our usual enemy. I can't shake the feeling there's a major bombshell headed our way, and we're going to be caught off guard with our thumbs up our asses." He leans back in his chair, feeling inadequate and emotionally spent. He realizes his situation report (SITREP) couldn't have had more holes of worthless information. "Boss, it's like being back in Iraq with boots on the ground and no Intel as to how to proceed. Our asses are literally hanging out, waiting for an RPG to park itself where the sun don't shine."

As we all take his information in, sending it twirling through our brains to be analyzed and scrutinized for its possibility, we sit in silence. I am the only one in the room who doesn't have a military background, so my analyzation is not driven by military-disciplined missions but instead from fighting an inhuman, vulgar enemy consisting of one. Only these men can relive their past service that landed them behind enemy lines; it's displayed within the nods passed between them. Only they understand the individual sacrifices that were made mentally and physically while watching each other's backs. Their unspoken, unconditional pledge of brotherhood has been earned on the battlefield. These men heard helicopter blades in the sky delivering salvation and relative safety, for they had brothers and sisters who would give their lives if need be to rescue them. But women who are trapped behind their own version of enemy lines are lucky if they hear wind chimes on a breezy day; no helicopter blades thump through their sky. They have to be rescued one at a time by Mickey's platoon, whose soldiers need to covertly launch an assault before the enemy even realizes they've infiltrated his world.

John reaches to the middle of the table and hits the com link to Dominic's cell. While it's ringing, he places the phone on speaker. "You got the Dom," a deep European drawl surges through the speaker.

"Dom, I've got Marco, Matt, and Reggie here with me. Do you have a SITREP?"

"Indeed, I do, Boss. The bastard is still pacing the parking lot like Matt explained to me this morning, but now he's attracting a lot of attention. I'm thinking a call to the local PD by an anonymous concerned citizen may be in order. I'm thinking when he sees a police cruiser pull into the parking lot heading in his direction, he should be scared off."

"I agree," John says. "Give them a call, and when he bolts, be sure to stay on him like dog crap to the soles of your boots." John disconnects the call and looks around the table, locking eyes with each of us in turn. After what seems like an eternity of silence, John says, "I don't think he believes Clarissa is still in there; I think he's waiting for Pix. She's the only common link to Clarissa's disappearance, except for Dr. Thadius, but Pix was the one in his face. He wants her. Marco, contact our security detail at the hospital and tell them I want a body following Pix every minute she's on duty, and she's in no way to leave the building without an escort. I'll contact her and my dad to let them know what we suspect and how we're going to proceed." He looks at me now, his eyes screaming for reassurances that he's doing the right thing. He lives the cruelty of being a dedicated leader, shouldering the rugged reality of his actions. Those actions have put one of our team in danger, again. But that's how our wars play out; they're always personal and incredibly human in so many unimaginable ways. You can't train for months on how to fight this enemy because there are too many variables. Every enemy we face is ironically driven by the same need to control and demoralize its victim, but that's where the comparison gets thrown way off kilter. No soldier of the devil handles losing his world of control the same; each one is unbelievably different with his unpredictability and level of anger. We start with some basics but have to change our plan of attack the closer we are to executing the mission. We have to figure out how each individual enemy thinks, how they will react to their territory being invaded and turned upside down. We know it will be dangerous on a multitude of levels, so we try to be prepared as best we can. But these soldiers have been trained well; we can't read every demented mind, and it sickens us that we have to try.

"John," I say, leaning in close. "I've watched Pix work and honestly believe that once you warn her of our suspicions, she'll take them to heart. Granted, this is a different enemy than she's used to, but I saw her actions yesterday with Benjamin—she knows he's dangerous!" I let him absorb my words as Suzie inches closer to him, ready to lend support in her own way. He places his hand on Suzie's back and gives me a nod of agreement. "John, you trained her to be one of your elite. She's smart and capable, even if she isn't looking through the scope of a sniper rifle."

After John reaches out to Pixie and his father to fill them in, there's nothing else to do except wait for Dominic's plan to play out. I look up and through the glass walls, I see Clarissa and Xander walk toward the medical bay. Xander is making sure there is enough space between them, so she feels comfortable. His hands are clasped behind his back, and his head is inclined as he speaks to her. I see a hesitant smile form on her lips and note the slight shrug of her shoulders. Her hair is still wet from her shower, so I'm assuming she didn't get a nap yet. Suzie is watching her also and gives me a slight whimper, asking if she can go. "Not yet, Suz, she needs a checkup first," I say, giving her a kiss on the top of her head. Xander will complete her medical assessment before we can move forward. Once we have that, we can formulate a workout focusing on strength training, both physically and mentally.

"Matt, why don't you grab a shower and some shut-eye? You've earned it," John says after watching his brother practically nod off at the table.

"Sounds good, Boss. You'd think we would get used to this shit after all this time."

"There's too much at stake for these women. We have to fight for them as well as keep ourselves safe. That's a lot on our shoulders."

"Have a good sleep, Matt," I say. "I think Suzie and I will do the same in a few, right, Suz?"

Chapter 25

Before Suzie and I leave, Marco lets us all know that Benjamin's truck is moving. Dominic's call to the local cops must have worked. We all look up to the monitor on the wall behind Marco and watch the GPS in full color. Benjamin's truck is the green icon traversing the city streets, and the yellow icon is Dominic following at a slight distance. Even if Dom loses him at a light or misses a turn, he has the same GPS info on his handheld screen, so we always have eyes on him.

After another fifteen minutes or so of following Benjamin's truck on the monitor, he comes to a stop. Dom sends us a quick text saying he has parked in front of his landscaping business and has gone inside. "Roger that," John replies. And on that note, I head to the Bunk House to grab a quick shower and find some clean clothes. I keep bins of extra supplies for myself and Suzie stashed under my favorite bunk. I have come to think of this as my home base, a place to recharge, re-stock, and interact a bit with others. I often need to remind myself that in order to be comfortable around people, I really should *be* around people.

Chapter 26

After three days, we rapidly become consumed with the endless monotony of Benjamin's surveillance. At this point, we would be happy watching him just take a walk or even stroll out to his mailbox. His routine is boring, causing all of us to be on edge watching what we know is the calm before the storm. The only change to the routine is how we are handling the surveillance on our end. We now have two teams of two made up of Matt and Gill on the day shift and Dominic and Oscar-D on the evening shift. Marco continues to monitor the feed on Benjamin's safe when he is home to give the guys a heads-up if he retrieves one of the weapons we know he has inside. That leaves John and I to dissect all decisions that need to be made, are safe, and the best options for all, especially our guys in the field. We are constantly roughing out different scenarios of action if they are needed.

Benjamin's routine starts each morning by leaving the house at 7:30 a.m., where he drives to the same coffee stand on his way to work. Once at work, he puts in a 7.5-hour day, which is followed by hitting the same greasy spoon drive-through, and as far as his detail can tell, he orders the same thing—a super-sized #6. From there, he heads to the hospital, where he does a slow drive-through of the parking lot and then parks where he can have a clear view of the employee entrance. We now have no doubt that he is watching for Pixie. But while he watches the entrance for her, Dom and Oscar-D are watching him from a good visibility spot a few cars away. He stays until he sees Pixie come through the door and head for her car, but he never attempts to confront her in any way. Once she leaves the parking lot, he drives to his favorite bar, where he stays until exactly 11:00 p.m., then drives directly home, never deviating from his route. This precise routine is scary enough to keep us in a semi-panic state at the Club House and is really screwing with the surveillance team's heads. Oscar-D keeps asking the Boss to give him a long leash so he can push Benjamin into making his move. But he's shot down each time, being told we still need to watch and let Benjamin play this out. Oscar-D even went so far as to tell John if he let him off his leash, that when this was over, he could personally shave off all his beautiful dreads.

One of the issues John and I were trying to deal with was Pixie's adamant refusal of changing her schedule to make it harder for Benjamin to become her stalker. Ever since she was informed of the fact he was watching her, she became insistent on becoming bait for Clarissa's freedom. This maniac needed to be destroyed, and as long as he was fixated on her, that gave Clarissa the much-needed time to heal physically. Then she can take the first steps of her journey, beginning the emotional struggle she will endure for what will seem like an eternity. She wants to draw him out, tease him into coming at her. She wants so bad to show him her inner huntress. She wants him to choke on his fear as he realizes the tables have been turned and he is now someone's *bitch*. She's been taught and knows firsthand that there are times you need to confront the enemy head-on, and she is so ready for the confrontation. She's aware of the risks and is comforted in the knowledge that the surveillance details have her back; they are a part of her—they are family. She wants so much to give Clarissa the chance to be reunited with her real family and to find a new one on her own terms.

It's the third night of surveillance, and the weather has taken a cold turn. Snow is beginning to show up in flurries here and there, causing drivers to act like they have never seen it before. The wintry forecast indicates it is just the beginning and that the Seattle area will be hit by a snow front coming out of Alaska, and temperatures will continue to drop through the night.

The snow begins to fall in earnest as Dominic and Oscar-D are parked outside the bar watching the door as patrons wander in and out. The light that streaks out through the door as it opens shows the surprise on the faces of patrons who are heading out. They look up at the sky in surprise as the cold flakes hit their faces and dance around their feet. It's always a terrible combination of alcohol and idiot drivers on the first snowfall of the year. It makes a person wonder how many accidents these drunks will cause, and hope that if they do cause one, they're the only ones to be hurt. But as we all know, *you can't fix stupid!!!*

After another fifteen minutes, Dominic's phone lights up, and the cab of the truck is filled with the lyrics from Toby Keith's "American Soldier," indicating the Boss is calling. "You got the Dom,

Boss, and may I say before you ask, yes, he's going to lose his shit any minute now. I'm begging you to take him up on his offer. Please, I'm freakin' begging you, let him off his leash because I'm getting really close to strangling him with it. Besides, he may look good bald. I'll hold him down, and you can shear off the dreads. Could be very therapeutic for both of us, especially me!!!"

"Put me on speaker," John says with resignation. "Reggie is here with me, and she thinks it would be smart to at least hear him out. Kid, I hope I don't regret this, but what do you have in mind? And if we decide it's worth the risk, you will have to be pulled from the detail. Are you good with that?"

"If anyone cares, I'm really... good with that," Dom interjects.

"Affirmative, Boss, I'm down with that. I thought I would head into the bar and scope it out on my way to the restroom. My plan is to order a beer..."

"Are you fucking kidding me??? I should shoot you right now," Dom's voice booms through the speakers, causing us to jump slightly. "Can I shoot him, Boss???"

"Hold on now, Dominator, just listen. The beer is to give me the chance to scope things out, see who's in there, and maybe be able to make some kind of contact with Benjamin. Maybe strike up a conversation, and if he's had a few, maybe I can get him talking. I want to poke the bear a little and get him all riled up and shit. Maybe that will drive him into making his move."

"Seriously, Dominator," I whisper quietly to John with a what-the-hell smile.

"I still want to shoot him, Boss!"

"Me too," John says through a clenched jaw. "Maybe later." He looks at his watch where it registers 9:50 p.m. "Okay, if you're going to do this, you better get in there. If he sticks to his routine, you've only got a little over an hour. I want audio from the minute you enter, so get your app up on your phone so we can have your back." Even with that said, John continues with the concern of a leader, "Be careful, brother."

"Roger that, Boss. Don't miss me too much, Dominator," he says before getting out of the truck.

"Seriously, Boss, we need to get that bozo committed or at least on some meds, but I think it would be easier to just…"

"Shoot him, yes, we know," John and I say in unison.

And this is why, once again, we know Oscar-D should fly solo.

Chapter 27

The snow continues to fall all night as promised yesterday, causing havoc on the roads where the plows couldn't keep up with it. With a ride from her personal driver, Michael, Abby has made it in to continue her sessions with Clarissa. After her arrival, she is informed by Michael and John that she is to find a bunk and get comfortable because she isn't leaving until the roads are clear. The stitches have been removed from Clarissa's head, and the bruises have begun to fade. The magic of foundation is able to cover them for the most part, letting us see how beautiful she is. Abby can now get the pictures for Clarissa's new identification, and with the help of Photoshop, they can continue to establish an identity to match. Clarissa decided to cut her hair and darken it, adding some soft highlights. Abby knows how I feel about what they discuss and what Clarissa will decide to do and where she will go. She knows I can't be involved with the decisions or even want to know them; I have to let go at this point. That's one of the ways I handle this job—knowing when to let go, and this is where I choose to do it. Yes, I will say goodbye; I will wish her well, remind her she will never be alone, and tell her she deserves to be happy. She deserves to be a *survivor.*

After Oscar-D was let off his leash last night, he was immediately replaced on the evening surveillance detail by Matt, who was more than happy to make the swap. He had no doubt Oscar-D would get things stirred up, and there was going to be some action going down soon.

John, Marco, and I are seated with Oscar-D and Dominic in the conference room as Pixie walks in and sits down beside me. She is immediately greeted by her new furry friend, who expects lavish praise for the bright smile she is showing. We are waiting for Matt to arrive so we can all listen to the audio feed from last night. When he arrives, John nods to Marco, who runs his magical fingers across the keyboard of his laptop, pushing the audio into the room.

"I was able to edit the audio enough to suppress a lot of the background noise, including the toilet flush, which was the first thing I heard," Marco says dryly without looking up from his screen.

"Hey, Boss, you said turn on the ears as soon as I went through the door!"

"Anyway," Marco continues, "as soon as I was done editing, I put the audio to paper to make it easier to follow. There are copies in the middle of the table if you want one. The first voice you hear is that of the bartender."

BARTENDER: "What'll it be?"

OSCAR-D: "Corona and keep-'em comin'!"

BARTENDER: "That bad, huh?"

OSCAR-D: "Wife trouble, need I say more?"

"This is where I take the stool next to Benjamin," Oscar-D interjects.

OSCAR-D: "Thanks, friend. Here's to wishin' I could beat the shit out of Darlene, that's my wife. What about you, brother? Wife trouble or just in a fuckin' bad mood?"

BENJAMIN: "What? Sorry, say again?"

OSCAR-D: "I said, is that look you're wearin' because you have woman troubles too?"

We hear more noise and glasses clinking close by but wait for a reply.

BENJAMIN: "Something like that."

OSCAR-D: "I don't know what Darlene got in her head lately—well, I do know. Her sister Sharlene been droppin' by, fillin' her empty head with ideas. Darlene been sassin' me terrible, sayin' things like; no more cookin', cleanin', or bumpin' until I start treatin' her right. What the hell is up with that, I ask ya?"

BENJAMIN: "Sounds like you need to show her who's boss, you know, tune her up a bit, put her in her place if you know what I mean? And get rid of that sister!"

OSCAR-D: "You got some experience with sassy women, I guess!"

BENJAMIN: "Yep, I'm dealing with something right now, actually!"

Right then we hear a strange snap come through the system.

OSCAR-D: "What the hell, man, no need for a blade. We're just havin' a conversation here!"

BENJAMIN: "Oh, this isn't for you—or my wife, for that matter!"

OSCAR-D: "Well, that's good to know. Because, damn, you could do a lot of damage with that thing!"

BENJAMIN: "This is for a meddling little blonde bitch, who won't be a problem much longer!"

OSCAR-D: "I see. So, what's your plan for blondie?"

BENJAMIN: "Why you so interested? Sounds like you got your own problems, pal."

We hear the snap again, and Oscar-D lets us know the knife is being closed.

BENJAMIN: "She's your property, pal. You own her, so you take the bumpin' whenever you want it, don't wait for her to give it as some kind of reward. You need to shut her off from everyone and everything, and if she doesn't comply, use the family as leverage to keep her in line. Let her know that there isn't anything you won't do to her, or anywhere you won't find her if she tries to run. And here's some good advice; when you're taking control, don't cause so much damage she ends up in the hospital where there are people who think they're heroes. I recently made that mistake, and I'm now trying to fix it. Are you catching on now, pal? Do you see the picture I just painted for you? If not, you can continue to come in here and complain about Darlene and stay the fuckin' pussy you are!"

Then we hear Benjamin ask for the check and tell the bartender to put the Pussy's drink on his tab. The audio goes silent, and we all turn to Pix, waiting for her reaction to what we just heard. She looks as mauled emotionally and exhausted physically as the rest of us. The last ten days have given none of us even a small time frame of refuge from the escalating fears we carry. It has been overly taxing being continually on alert, especially for her. I could feel Pix's raw emotions from across the table, her inner hatred for the man escalating with each hour that passes waiting for Benjamin's blow to come. At least now we have something tangible, knowing Oscar-D poked the bear as he intended. But it's a two-sided coin of reality; heads, he makes his move soon; tails, we end up waiting for days in purgatory.

"Okay, kid," John says. "Get some sleep, and when you get up, we'll need you on monitor surveillance, backing up the teams from here. And, kid, you did good."

"The Pussy appreciates the praise," Oscar-D says, laughing as he heads for the door but stops and turns around. "You guys know I'm really not a Pussy, right?"

"GO!!!!!"

I look at Pix, and before I can even open my mouth, she puts up her hand, stopping me from saying what she thinks I'm going to. "No, not happening," she says with an angered determination.

I sigh at her reaction. I knew she was done listening to me or anyone, for that matter, so it didn't surprise me when she shut me down before I uttered a word. But this time, she was wrong about what was coming. "All I was going to say was you've heard what he has in mind and to be careful. I know you can take care of yourself, sister." She's frustrated with herself and on edge from a lack of sleep, not to mention the information she just absorbed. The weight of the unknown causing her shoulders to visibly collapse in on her, making her look even smaller than normal as she stands to leave. So all she manages to do is nod her head with an acknowledgment, pleading with her eyes for me to understand where she's coming from, and of course, I do. I look at John as she leaves, sitting up straighter in my chair, and tell him I'm glad she was covering his ass in Iraq. He agrees, knowing for a fact he wouldn't be here if it weren't for her.

Chapter 28

To say that we're all anxious is a laughable understatement. To say that we're all hoping Benjamin will make a move on Pix is despicably outrageous, bordering on sadistic. But here we sit behind the curtain, safely tucked away, looking forward to the danger we have allowed her to seek. She is our sacrifice to Benjamin, our gift to him served up on a silver platter, and if that isn't the epitome of sick, I don't know what is. All we can do is silently wallow in our atrocious actions as we send one of our own into the fray. What does that say about the people we have turned into? I think it's a testimony to what we allow ourselves to endure for the sake of others. It comforts me as I begin to shut my mind down at night because we know that in no way will we feel we need to justify our actions. We feel no need for atonement, for we have done nothing wrong; we each carry a clear conscience. I feel confident in speaking for the rest of my team, for we know that if we didn't do what we do, there would be even more evil in this world.

Just thinking about it pushes me on, drives me to try and find the head of the snake and remove it harshly, but all the while knowing it's a futile endeavor because it will just grow another. We will never win, but we will keep finding ways to slow it down.

Then what we have all been waiting for suddenly comes crashing down, and it is worse than any scenario we could have come up with. What we have sickly been hoping for has happened: Benjamin made his move, and Pix is down!! Yes, the waiting is over, but at what cost?

I had just finished with Suzie's bath and was toweling her off when we both noticed the atmosphere in the Club House had changed dramatically. I turn around and see John running through the maze of workstations in my direction. I know instantly shit has just hit the fan, but have no idea how bad the said shit is until he reaches the Bunk House. He fills me in on what little information he has: Pix has been stabbed multiple times and is losing a lot of blood. That leaves both of us to question where her security detail was and how on earth Matt and Dominic lost sight of Benjamin long enough for him to attack her.

The lights inside the Medical Bay have been turned on, illuminating its sterile interior, and I can see Xander shouting orders to all the medical staff. There is an obnoxious red strobe light positioned above the entrance from the motor pool, indicating a team member is down, and time is of the essence. The soft lighting that is normally illuminating the computer monitors from above is now a glaring bright presence, casting its sharpness upon everyone below as they are all on alert. I am on my own level of high alert at this point as I follow John toward the entrance of the motor pool. I feel Suzie glue her wet nose to my back pocket, positioning herself as close as she can to render her support as we wait what seems like hours for Matt to arrive with Pix. Looking over my shoulder, I see each team member is showing body language full of agitation as they try to stay focused on their duties. They aren't enduring the waiting any better than we were. If one of us is down, we're all down.

John turns and screams at Marco, "Where the hell is Benjamin, and is Dominic on his ass?" But before Marco has a chance to reply, we see vehicle headlights glaring at us through one of the back windows of the motor pool.

"They're here," Oscar-D announces, at least I think it was him. With all the commotion, it was hard to tell.

"Get the gurney ready, and everyone clear the way," Xander barks. We all comply and part like the Red Sea so the medical team can push forward.

Suzie and I are still standing behind John at this point. I can see the muscles in his arms twitching to the max as he does his best to stay put and out of the way. And I'm not doing much better as I realize my fists are clenched so tightly, my nails are turning my palms bloody from the small punctures. I don't even react except to wipe both my hands on my jeans.

"Marco!!!" I hear John shout above all the activity. "God damn it, Marco!!!" he yells again when he didn't get a response the first time. Standing behind him, I can see his body tense with each shout, his chest rumbling with anger as he lets loose his concern for Pix. He feels helpless, standing on the sidelines as one of his team is bleeding out because of this war we fight.

"Dom has him, Boss. The road's a mess because of the snow, but he's got him."

That's all that registers in my mind as I watch the gurney whiz by full of blood and Pix squirming in the middle of it. The sticky blood trail is heavy from the motor pool into the Med Bay, and running right through the middle of it is Matt, covered from head to toe with the crimson liquid that was once flowing through Pix. The Security Guard is slowly following Matt while covering the back of his head with a cloth that one of the nurses has given him. What the hell happened to him, I wonder. He isn't too steady on his feet. There were so many details that needed to be filled in, but all the focus was on Pix right now, exactly where it should be.

"Pix!!! Pix!!!" Clarissa's voice comes traveling through the Club House as she runs toward us with Abby close behind her. Before anyone thought to stop her, she runs up to the glass walls surrounding the Medical Bay, where she can see all too clearly what is happening. She screams again and slaps the glass with both open palms, tears streaming down her face.

"What happened???" Abby looks from John to me, hoping we have some answers, but all we can say is we don't know the details yet.

"All we know right now is she's been stabbed. We need to speak to Matt, and then we'll have a better picture of the events." She nods with understanding and moves to try to give comfort to Clarissa because she's still crying with her hands and face glued to the glass wall. I look into the Medical Bay and see Matt, all bloody and estranged, sliding down the wall next to the door. He wipes his eyes with blood-soaked hands, and his body begins to shake. All he can do is hold his head in his hands as he is racked with emotion. My heart goes out to him as I witness again just how much we are all invested in the life we have chosen. John enters through the glass door and kneels down next to him, pulling him into a brotherly embrace, indicating with a nod to the nurse who is waiting to give Matt a shot to calm him down. The same nurse then turns to the Security Guard and motions to the chair in the corner, where I am assuming she will be assessing his head injury and possibly giving him some stitches. I know we have to question both of them to find out what happened, but I think giving them a few minutes seems like the right thing to do right now. Besides, we still don't know how Pix is doing. Xander is working swiftly to stop the bleeding and assess her injuries. He screams for more blood to be hung while gently rolling her onto her side to see if there is any damage to her back. I think back to when

Xander suggested each team member donate their own blood for just this situation. I called him a vampire but realize now it was brilliant.

We wait a few more minutes, watching Xander and his staff working to get Pix's bleeding under control but realize it will be a while before any update will be coming. Besides, I've seen enough blood to last me two lifetimes. After the nurse is finished with the Security Guard's injury, John motions for him to follow us into the conference room, grabbing Marco on the way. "Can you get the surveillance feed from the hospital up on the screen?" John says as calmly as he can to Marco. Lucky for us, about three years ago, the hospital installed cameras to cover the employee entrance from the back parking lot. They were getting so many complaints from the staff, mostly female staff, about leaving after shift in the dark and not feeling safe walking to their cars.

"I'm working on it, Boss, almost got it." We wait to see the screen behind him come to life as Matt staggers in, still bloody but a little less agitated now because of the shot he was given. The video is forgotten for now.

"I'm so sorry, Boss. I couldn't get there any faster! Dom and I were following him as usual, and as usual, we knew where he was going. But the freakin' snow on the road caused two cars in front of us to slide into each other, blocking us before we could move into the left turn lane to enter the hospital parking lot. Dom tried to quickly go around them, but then the idiot in the car in the left turn lane tried to overcorrect and ended up blocking that lane also. SHIT!!! SHIT!!!!! Benjamin had already made it through the light to turn left into the hospital, but we were trapped. I jumped out and took off through traffic, barely able to keep from slipping on the ice while dodging oncoming cars to get to the parking lot." He begins to cry again, visibly fighting not to break down completely so he can finish telling us what happened. Watching this man discernibly crumble before our eyes was heartbreaking, and if Pix doesn't make it, he will never forgive himself. He won't find comfort in the fact we can't predict the weather. And even with everything we've dealt with in the past, he will forget that the unpredictability of others is a given. No, he will carry this darkness forever. "When I finally made it to the parking lot and was just a few cars away, I saw Benjamin. He lifted his hand, and in the illumination of the parking lot lights, there was a flash of silver that registered all too fast in my mind. I swear I tried to get to him, I swear I did," he delivers while shoving his palms into his eyes as if to keep the tears contained. "But it all happened so fast. I didn't follow him because Pix was—she was down but conscious, looking at me with those huge blue eyes of hers. I was going to get her to the emergency department there, but she said no, she needed to come here. She kept saying she didn't tell him anything just before she passed out. Then I see Tom getting up from the ground a few yards away," he indicates with his head in the direction of the Security Guard, "and he said he would drive after he helped me get Pix into the car." He starts to tremble in earnest at this point, pushing his palms into his eyes again. "I can't count how many times she had our backs over there. We failed her!!! I failed her!!!" His declaration hangs in the air as he pulls a chair out from the table, folding himself into it, waiting like a child for the punishment he feels he deserves. At this point, John doesn't respond; it would be futile to try.

"What about you?" John asks while turning to Tom.

"It all happened so fast. Pix and I were going through the door, commenting on how much it had snowed and wondering if the parking lot was going to be slick or not. She was a couple steps ahead of me, and then all of a sudden, I'm seeing stars and kissing the asphalt through cold snow. I didn't go completely out, but I couldn't move. Then it was pretty much a blur after that until I saw Matt leaning over her. That's when I was finally able to get my footing and stand. I was right behind her. I can't believe I didn't hear him come up behind me, and I have no idea what he clocked me with," he says, touching the back of his head gently. "I'm as sorry as can be about going down like that, Boss, really."

"Marco, start the feed," I say.

Our emotions are high, colliding with our pain of failure as we watch the screen portray pretty much what Matt and Tom have told us. We will keep this feed in-house for now, but will use it down the road as part of the message we will deliver to Benjamin. I don't know how Pix was able to keep her head while bleeding out in the parking lot, but she knew if Matt had taken her into the emergency department of the hospital, it could put Mickey in danger. Too many questions would have to be answered, not to mention a police report would be filed, putting not just Mickey but all of us in jeopardy in so many ways.

"Damn, we knew he had a knife from Oscar-D's recon job the other night—even Pix knew at this point. But she was taken off guard by the attack, and there was nothing we could do to prepare."

"Shit!!! Shit!!! Shit, we should have searched his truck for weapons when we slapped the tracker on it," John says while running his hands down his face. Not for the first time is John kicking himself for not being Superman, the mighty General Patton of Thurston County. The war he came home from and the one he came home to are always colliding in ways we civilians will never understand. The failures on home soil are harder to step around because they involve family. But he is only human, with human emotions that flare up, testing his strength. How he finds the resolve he needs to move forward, to carry on our fight from these front lines, is extraordinary, to say the least. None of us will be able to shake off what happened, but we will find a way to live with it and hopefully learn from it as well. Hindsight is a miserable bitch. It plays with your mind in ways that cut deep. We've all felt the pain at one point or another.

Chapter 29

We look out into the activity of the Club House and see that Abby has managed to pull Clarissa away from the Medical Bay, but only after Michael arrived and administered a sedative. She is still visibly upset but allows herself to be guided to a chair outside the glass walls, with Abby and Suzie there for comfort. Michael has joined Xander, and they're working swiftly, along with the capable hands of the nurses, to keep Pix alive. Their audience, watching through the glass, can do nothing but look on with strangled hope—the hope that our family will not suffer another blow. The obnoxious red strobe light had been turned off once Pix was wheeled in on the gurney, and the intense lighting above the tech's computer screens is once again casting a softer glow.

"Can you tell me where Benjamin is right now!?" John barks.

"I don't believe this, Boss," Marco says. "He's at the bar. He didn't run, he went to the *freakin'* bar as if nothing happened. What the hell! That's some messed up shit, man!!!"

"That's because his actions are that of an amorality personality disorder. He's capable of performing violent acts and feeling no guilt. To put it bluntly, he's a sociopath, so to him, he doesn't need to change his routine because he's done nothing wrong." As soon as the words are out of my mouth, I'm hit with the smoldering fire of my past weaknesses. My guilt slowly rears its ugly head once again from the stagnant water of the mental well I've dug. The walls of the well are jagged and sharp, the depth staggering, its purpose to drown the darkest parts of me. But my guilt is resilient and strong; it climbs to the top of the well and peeks over its edge, letting me know it still lurks in the liquid darkness, and I'm not rid of it yet. But I roughly push it back down, hoping it will acknowledge the same feeling of defeat I've had to. I want it to feel my resistance; I want it to suffer; I want it to know I can stand its taunts today better than yesterday, because I'm getting stronger. I'm determined not to lose any of the ground I've earned, so I slam the lid of the well shut with that earned determination.

My message is shocking even to me. I'm hoping it realizes I'm the one in control now, and only I can open the barrier. It wants me to stumble back from the progress I've made, but I fight it and stand firm, retracting my emotions to lock them in tight. I lived with my own sociopath and realize I fight him even now, even after all this time. He still flares up inside my head unexpectedly, trying to leach out the last ounce of my earned resolve. But I'm stronger now, and the guilt is fading on many levels, spending more and more time in the darkness at the bottom of the well. John watches the anger cross my face, sees the twitch of my jaw as shaking hands reach out for purchase to connect with the back of the chair in front of me. I can feel how much he wants to comfort; it's jumping off his entire body, but he's hesitant, and that saddens both of us. Just like Suzie, he always has my back. So when I look up into his concerned eyes, I am comforted by their understanding and somehow know my resolve to fight will only get stronger.

Without taking his eyes off of me, he says to Marco, "Confirm with Dom that he is actually there and let him know I'll send someone over to back him up."

"On it!"

We see Xander and Michael remove blood-covered surgical gloves and their masks before stepping out of the Medical Bay. Michael and Xander look right at us and indicate for us to join them. I can't tell by the looks they wear on their exhausted faces if this is going to be good news or not, so I try to keep my mind as blank as possible. As if that is going to happen, considering all the bloody towels and instruments I am watching the nurses start to clean up.

"For now, she's holding her own," Xander says. "She has three deep stab wounds to her lower abdomen that thankfully didn't cause any real damage to her internal organs. We were able to stop the internal bleeding and repair those, but she's lost a lot of blood. We've given her two pints of blood already and are hanging another one to replace what she's lost."

"I was able to stitch up the defensive wounds on her arms while Xander stitched up the others. I believe that her injuries to her abdomen would have been more extensive if she hadn't deflected the knife with her arms first. Luckily, she knew how to redirect the knife; otherwise, the damage would have been much worse. We're confident that she'll be fine. She will recover," Michael says while pulling Abby up from her chair to hold her close.

The ragged sobs we hear from Clarissa are so intense it's obvious she's losing what little control she was able to achieve after the sedative was given. Maybe it was wearing off now; maybe she needed another. "Clarissa," I hear Abby whisper after she sits back down beside her. "That's good news, honey. Pix is going to be fine."

"This time, Abby!!! But what about next time? Will it be you or Reggie next time? Maybe it will be my mother," she begins to shriek so loudly everyone in the Club House can hear her. All heads turn toward us as her tirade is delivered among emotional screams full of fear. "He's not going to stop! He will hunt me down, and if he can't find me, he could go after all of you!!! I can't allow that to happen. I have to go back so no one else gets hurt. Please, I have to go back!!!" Abby pulls her head to her shoulder, whispering softly into her hair, trying to say something that will comfort her, but right now, Clarissa doesn't want to hear it.

"Abby, will you take her to her room, maybe get her to lay down for a bit," I ask while everyone else is still reeling from her outburst.

John leans into me and says softly, "We have a problem here if we can't convince her that we're all safe, and that includes her mother."

"I really don't think she cares what happens to her anymore, John. She feels she needs to sacrifice her freedom, even her life, in order to keep us safe and outrun the guilt." I deliver the statement through a sadness as I try to describe the guilt she wears as an old, ill-fitting suit. I have that same suit, but have pulled it from its hanger in my closet and thrown it into the corner, where it waits to be tossed into the well and be destroyed alongside my own guilt and other weaknesses.

I'm like every mother on earth who can tune into the different nuances of their child's cries, knowing instantly what each one means. But the difference is, as they interpret the little human cries, I interpret my canine child's barks and whines. So when I hear Suzie cut loose with a frenzied monologue of extreme agitation, I know something is happening, and she needs me. John and I look up from our conversation in time to see Abby running after Clarissa as she heads toward the motor pool entrance. Suzie is pacing back and forth, waiting for me to come running, which I have a hard time doing, so I'm a few feet behind John as we head toward Suzie. "Mom, stop, we got this," John yells. When we make it to the entrance, all we see is Clarissa's back as she's running through the snow into the darkness.

"Go," I say to Suzie, who is off like a bullet flying toward her. John starts to head out also, but I hold him back with my hand on his chest.

"Why aren't we going after her? She's wearing nothing but slippers, and she has no coat on!"

"She's safe out there. Suzie is with her." I look at his face and see the question in his eyes as he tries to figure this out. My hand remains on his chest as I say, "She's trying to outrun the storm she feels she's brought down on us because of her decision to let us help her. She's overwhelmed and extremely fragile because of the raw guilt she feels right now. She will burn herself out soon enough trying to figure out exactly where she is and where she should go. Like you said, the elements will probably work in our favor. She is going to be freezing shortly. See how Suzie is actually herding her back this way without her even realizing it? The snow is causing her a lot of confusion. Trust me, she needs to have the destruction of that storm run her down like an emotional tornado before she can start to think straight."

We continue to stand in the entrance of the motor pool, watching the snow swirling through the security lights mounted above the door. The still silence of the snow allowing us to hear Suzie deliver her maternal comfort with small whines and cold nose touches as she keeps Clarissa heading our way. It doesn't take long for my expected outcome to be delivered. We see her drop to her knees, hitting the snow so hard she ends up covered with the cold softness she pushed up around her while doing so. We can see the breaths she takes between sobs as her feelings of hopelessness surround her while she screams into the silence. John takes my hand from his chest and squeezes it softly, "I think the storm has passed," he says, releasing my hand, leaving my fingers wanting the warmth back as he heads out to Clarissa. He bends down and scoops her up in his arms, holding her like the wounded animal she is. He lends comfort by his actions, and Suzie is more than happy to be his wingman, falling into step right beside him. I watch as his face fills with concern and notice his strong arms cradling Clarissa as he walks to me, and suddenly I can't help but wonder what it would feel like to be cradled in his arms like that. *Where the hell did that come from?*

He carries her in and doesn't put her down until he enters the Medical Bay and deposits her on a bed. She's trying to calm down, muttering her feelings of guilt for the danger she feels she has brought down on all of us. But there is nothing we can say right now to defuse those feelings. She's just going to have to trust us. It's true that if we never met her, Pix wouldn't have been hurt, but the rainstorm of danger she feels she is causing is one that hangs in the air, waiting for its chance to pour down on us every time we rescue someone. Unfortunately, this situation is normal for us.

John meets me outside the Medical Bay once he knows she's in good hands. Abby is there, by her side again, helping as much as she can. "If Benjamin continues his routine, he will leave the bar in about an hour. I'm getting a team together to take care of this bastard once he gets home. This ends tonight! He's made his move; now we make ours!"

"No!" I bark, "no team. This one is mine, and the only backup I need is Mountain, so make the call!"

"Reggie!"

"Make the call, John!!!" I say sharply, leaving no misunderstanding as to how serious I am as I stomp my way to the Bunk House, leaving him to glare helpless daggers into my back. The only thing I'm focused on right now is the fact that this *will* end tonight. He will definitely get *my* message. I feel Suzie's cold nose touch my hand as we enter the Bunk House. She knows all too well that I'm getting ready to walk into a situation that puts me in danger and her as well, but she doesn't even think about herself. Her job is to have my back, and she does it unconditionally. I feel so tired, physically and emotionally; this has been an extremely rough extraction for all of us, especially Clarissa and Pix. I can't help but think we may lose Pix after this, but I've seen this woman stand up to one of the Devil's minions and show no fear, so maybe she will stay with us. I silently acknowledge all the extremes we have faced while helping Clarissa, but I also acknowledge the parallels to my own story. I have started realizing my outlook on the future and my emotions are becoming induced with power. I feel like the dark cloud I have existed under for so long is drifting away and becoming lighter, because by helping Clarissa, I am helping myself as well.

in his arms like that. *Where the hell did that come from?*

He carries her in and doesn't put her down until he enters the Medical Bay and deposits her on a bed. She's trying to calm down, muttering her feelings of guilt for the danger she feels she has brought down on all of us. But there is nothing we can say right now to defuse those feelings. She's just going to have to trust us. It's true that if we never met her, Pix wouldn't have been hurt, but the rainstorm of danger she feels she is causing is one that hangs in the air, waiting for its chance to pour down on us every time we rescue someone. Unfortunately, this situation is normal for us.

John meets me outside the Medical Bay once he knows she's in good hands. Abby is there, by her side again, helping as much as she can. "If Benjamin continues his routine, he will leave the bar in about an hour. I'm getting a team together to take care of this bastard once he gets home. This ends tonight! He's made his move; now we make ours!"

"No!" I bark, "no team. This one is mine, and the only backup I need is Mountain, so make the call!"

"Reggie!"

"Make the call, John!!!" I say sharply, leaving no misunderstanding as to how serious I am as I stomp my way to the Bunk House, leaving him to glare helpless daggers into my back. The only thing I'm focused on right now is the fact that this *will* end tonight. He will definitely get *my* message. I feel Suzie's cold nose touch my hand as we enter the Bunk House. She knows all too well that I'm getting ready to walk into a situation that puts me in danger and her as well, but she doesn't even think about herself. Her job is to have my back, and she does it unconditionally. I feel so tired, physically and emotionally; this has been an extremely rough extraction for all of us, especially Clarissa and Pix. I can't help but think we may lose Pix after this, but I've seen this woman stand up to one of the Devil's minions and show no fear, so maybe she will stay with us. I silently acknowledge all the extremes we have faced while helping Clarissa, but I also acknowledge the parallels to my own story. I have started realizing my outlook on the future and my emotions are becoming induced with power. I feel like the dark cloud I have existed under for so long is drifting away and becoming lighter, because by helping Clarissa, I am helping myself as well.

Chapter 30

As I enter the Bunk House, I'm grateful for its emptiness; I need to focus on tonight and what I'm going to do. I sit down on my bunk and am suddenly struck with an exhaustion that not only begs my body to surrender to its yearning, it wants my emotions as well. I feel Suzie jump up onto the bed and take her position beside me, looking into my eyes, she sees what's floating around in my head and lets me know she's there to protect me. I look at my watch and realize we have some time before Benjamin will head home. My stomach churns with hatred as I picture the message I'll deliver—the message I need to deliver—and as usual, I will not second guess myself. Maybe I would have second thoughts as to the severity of punishment I have planned if my morals weren't so screwed up, my humanity needing to decide who is good and who is evil. But I have dissected my human decency many times, so I have no doubts concerning my inner thoughts and plans for tonight. I know in this darkness of reality that my actions will be just. I realized a long time ago that the recipe for human behavior isn't just blended between good and evil. My morals and my humanity have taken a huge hit, but their condition no longer taunts me from within the confines of my being. In my world, morals and humanity are overrated. So, I had no choice but to throw my jaded morals and humanity into a "MORALS BLENDER." The instructions I followed are these: I threw in the morals and humanity I had before I was destroyed, followed by the morals and humanity I was left with after I was destroyed and pushed the pulse button. When the cocktail was finished blending, I removed the top and looked inside, hoping I would get some insight. And I did—the insight I needed was floating on top. I made my decision and drank the blended mixture like a desperate drunk decides to drink mouthwash. And I never looked back. I can live with my cocktail of low morals and humanity because I believe it is a just concoction. I have earned every ounce of that concoction and can definitely live with my actions. I will not let the guilt I have consume or define me any longer. I've worked too long and hard to move forward. I'm so tired, I'm so close...

His blood trail is fresh, its scent filling my nose with rage and the need for vengeance as I chase him through the cold snow. I'm like a wolf drawn to his scent, the smell of fear is dripping from every pore in his body. This time, he's the prey, and I'm hungry for revenge... I scream through the night for him to stop; it's the only sound pushing through the silence caused by the blanket of snow. He looks back at me and can see I'm closing in, so he tries to run faster, but the snow is slowing him down, and the blood trail is getting darker. A smile crosses my face as I continue to pursue him through the accumulating blanket of white.

I catch a glimpse of something out of the corner of my eye. I don't want to take a second to look, but all of a sudden, it's there in my path, something small and bleeding. Then I realize if I don't stop, I will run right over it. Breathing hard, I look down but then immediately look after my prey; I still see him, but he's gaining ground. DAMN!! The small creature is bleeding into the snow. It's surrounded by the contrast of crimson on white. I hear a meow—it's a kitten. My mind suddenly realizes this is Clarissa's kitten from her past. Without thinking, I scoop it up with my left hand because my right hand holds the bat. The sight of this small creature and the obvious pain it is feeling further enrages my resolve to punish this man, so I kick up the speed, wishing I actually had four legs like the wolf, and push myself harder.

"I'm close now. I can see the fear on his face and smell the panic oozing from his body as he looks over his shoulder at me. I'm close, so close. All the years of living within the dominate bubble of violence are pushing me forward. All the minutes, days, weeks, and years of fear, of pain and shame I endured will be vindicated in just a few more yards. I'm close, so close. But suddenly, suddenly he falls. Suddenly he is no longer breathing. Suddenly the hope I had to end him with my own hands is taken from me, AGAIN!!!! No! No! I scream at him to come back. I need to finish this, you son of a bitch. I need to finish you, I say and swing the bat, and swing the bat, and swing the bat down onto his bloody body until I can no longer lift my arm from the exhaustion driven by hate. But that doesn't fill the need I have to continue to swing the bat!!!! I stand over the bloody bastard, watching as the snow falls to mingle with his blood, making a hissing sound as it connects with the heat he carries from his home in hell. His dark armor of evil no longer protects him as his soul screams for life, reaching for the forgiveness he needs from his creator."

I feel a heaviness on my chest and warm breath skimming my face as Suzie calms me, letting me know she's here.

"Reggie, Reggie," I hear from a soft whisper, "I'm here."

The tunnel of sleep starts to fade, and I feel a strange awareness as I listen intently, trying to figure out who is saying my name. There it is again, delivered softly next to my ear. I'm being lifted up to a sitting position and feel strong arms hold me close. I open my eyes slowly and see John looking directly into my eyes, his face just inches from mine. Years of running from any kind of physical closeness tells me to pull back and fold into myself, so that's what I try to do, but notice my resolve to do so isn't as strong as before. He holds my chin tenderly with his hand, not allowing me to turn away. He smells of Irish Spring, but reeks of MAN, a gentle man. *Where the hell is that coming from right now?*

The room is silent as he continues to hold me, the only light a soft glow from a lamp in the corner.

"I see you, Reggie, the real you, the one you hide behind this," he says and tenderly runs his thumb down the scar that destroyed my cheek. I'm letting him touch me, hold me close, and it feels unreal. Maybe I'm still dreaming. If so, I don't want to wake up yet. "Reggie, you think carrying around your guilt is your destiny, but it's not. Haven't you atoned for what you think was weakness? It's time to let it go. You've tortured yourself long enough. These scars don't need to define you!" I don't tense up when he pulls my head into his chest, cupping the back of my neck gently. It feels good and natural. I can't get enough of his warmth and his smell as he continues to whisper assurances into my hair. I must still be dreaming...

I lift my head and look directly at him, my eyes delivering a message of agreement into his as I let the tears begin to flow. "I'm close, John. I really am. But in order to unlock the door of the prison I've put myself in, I need to deliver this message tonight—me, not a team. It's like I'm pulling on a thread to form the opening of what could have been, and in doing so, I'm unraveling and destroying what has been. Ever since we met Clarissa, I have realized that this is somehow my opportunity to destroy my guilt, or at least get close. There's a knot in the string that I need to untie, a barrier still left to bypass. This sad case has finally given me the clarity I've been looking for. Every time I look at Benjamin Troy, I don't see Benjamin Troy, I see *him*." He knows exactly who *him* represents, and I feel his body tense and his hands, still positioned possessively on my lower back, begin to shake. "I'm doing this as much for myself as Clarissa," I say softly.

"I'm coming with you, no arguments," he says harshly, but immediately regrets it. "I'm sorry, I didn't mean to spit that in your face. I just want to be there for you. Reggie, there are things I need to do also. I hope you can understand that."

I do understand, but this is something I need to do alone. So I try a different tactic to get him to realize that in order for me to move forward, I have to put the past to rest in my own way. "John," I say and slowly reach up between us to lay my hand on his strong chest. "If you see me, really see me in here," I say and pull my hand from his chest to place it over my heart, "then you know why I need to do this myself." It takes a few strong heartbeats, but he finally acknowledges my words with a resigned nod, his eyes drilling his reluctant understanding into mine. Then suddenly, everything shifts around me as I allow him to lean in and kiss my lips softly, and it's wonderful that there's no panic or need for retreat skipping into my thoughts. It is warm and wonderful, a natural act that won't be followed by darkness and pain. An act I hadn't realized I'd been missing, a craving gently sated, delivered on a silent promise of closeness and trust. We break the kiss, letting our foreheads touch as both of us feel connected to each other in a way neither of us expected. How long has he felt this way and I didn't notice? How long would he have waited? But before I can ask, we are smothered in a wet tongue from you know who. Apparently, she'd been sitting demurely watching the show, enjoying herself immensely, and now she's letting us know she approves.

Chapter 31

"Did you get ahold of Mountain?" I ask John as he gets up and heads to the door.

"Yes, he's on his way. I'd still like to send a detail along, at a distance, if you don't mind?" He looks at me with a road map of emotions crossing his face. He's wondering if he's making a mistake by letting me go without him. But he knows if we're to move forward personally, he can't push it; he's waited so long to get to this point. The man knows me that well, and it makes me care for him even more. Things are seriously different between us now; it's nice, so I agree to a distant detail. A compromise we both can live with.

"I'll be fine, John," I say and give a nod. "I'm going to get my things together as soon as I check on Clarissa. I want her to know it's almost over." I pull myself up and stand next to the bed, turning his way with a shyness that I haven't felt since childhood. His smile is all I need to prove I'm wide awake and not dreaming after all, one step closer to being a survivor.

I step up to Clarissa's room and see Abby curled up in a cushioned chair beside the bed. Even in sweatpants and barefoot, she is elegant. How does she do that? She's reading a book in the soft light from the small lamp on the nightstand, and I know she will be there all night, because that's who she is. Clarissa appears to be sleeping, so I whisper from the door, "How's she doing?"

"She finally drifted off a little bit ago. I hope she sleeps through the night now. John was looking for you earlier, did he find you?"

Oh boy, did he, I want to say but answer with a nod and a yes. "I'm leaving shortly to deliver our message to Benjamin. It's something I need to do myself. This case has caused me to actually listen to the speeches I have given to all our Rescues concerning moving on and forgiving yourself for real or imagined issues. I'm beginning to feel like I've tortured myself long enough. I'm ready to forgive my past, but I need some closure. Honestly, I've realized as much as we've helped this woman," I say and point to Clarissa, "her case has helped me more. Like I told John, I don't see Benjamin Troy when I look at him; I see someone else who needs to feel my anger. This message is my message, and it's been a long time coming. I need to deliver it myself in order to move forward."

"Reggie, please know that we have always loved you, and even if this message doesn't give you the closure you need, we will help you find it. We love you; we're your family." She looks at me from across the room as she uncurls her legs from the chair and leans forward. "But my son loves you in a totally different way…" She's waiting for my reaction; I can see her holding her breath, hoping I know what she means.

"I was just made aware of that," I say shyly. "How did I not see it, Abby?"

"Because you weren't ready. You needed to love yourself first; then you'd be able to let someone else do the same. Promise me you'll be safe out there, doing what's necessary for Clarissa and yourself. I believe you when you say this is what you've waited for; this is how to get some closure and peace. You've kept yourself locked away for far too long, telling yourself you didn't deserve to be happy. But you do deserve to be happy, Reggie; you deserve to be able to move forward with a clear conscience and feel free of your past. You deserve to know what real love feels like."

Chapter 32

As I walk out of the Bunk House with Suzie trailing just steps behind me, I see John and Mountain in a deep conversation. John is doing most of the talking, and as usual, Mountain is acknowledging the instructions with a nod of his head, standing tall with his arms crossed over his chest. To say they were in a deep conversation is a bit overstated because, as always, John was the only one talking. John stands a little over six feet tall, but Mountain makes him look short, as he is at least eight or nine inches taller. He is a silent giant, built like a slab of granite, who wears a look of fierceness to hide the sadness he carries inside. His hair is long and blonde, which he pulls back into a ponytail at the back of his neck, reminding me of Trace Adkins, the country singer and actor. He even rides a Harley like Trace did in the movie "The Lincoln Lawyer" with Matthew McConaughey. Mountain's story is one we are all aware of; he had done time in prison for killing his sister's abuser after he found her dead by his hands. When he was released from prison, John approached him concerning joining Mickey. Mountain is a fellow military brother, even though it was in an unrecognized branch of service. He is a Merchant Marine through and through. Mountain agreed to join us but only if John told the team everything about him first. He wasn't going to hide anything from us; he gave no apologies for his actions. I felt comfortable around him immediately; maybe it was because we both were locked up for so long—him behind real bars and me behind the bars of fear. A different kind of cage, but one that restricted us from living.

Suzie whines as she sees them, and I let her go say hello. She loves Mountain, and as far as I know, she is the only one to bring a smile to his sad features. After the affection to Suzie is complete, he stands and says, "Evening, Miss Reggie."

"Thank you for having my back on this, Mountain; I have a feeling it's going to be a tough one."

"I'll be in the motor pool when you're ready," he says and turns, calling Suzie to follow. I give her the okay, and she scampers off, leaving me to say my goodbyes to John. We look at each other in a way that shouts it's almost over, but there's also a promise of something more. All I want to do is reach out and touch him, bring him close, and assure him I'll be back and on my way to becoming whole again. But I don't reach out, and I can't speak. All I can do is soak up the new emotions.

I do manage a smile and nod before I turn to leave, but he stops me with his hand on my shoulder and leans in close. "I'll be right here the whole time you're out there, and yes, I will worry, just like I always have. But you need to understand that no matter how long it takes, you're going to let me in here," he points to my heart, making sure there is no confusion. "I mean it, no matter how long it takes. Sadly, this horrible evil we fight has brought us together to form an even stronger resolve to push its darkness in ways it never dreamed of. You and I will be a force to be reckoned with, a team in more ways than one." I listen with my heart, which is something foreign to me, as you know, so my response is a lonely tear running down my cheek. I try to say something, but my throat is swollen with emotion. He reaches out to wipe the salty tear from my face and smiles. I find myself leaning into his palm and returning his smile with my own. I step back from the warmth of his touch and nod my head in agreement before turning to join Mountain in the motor pool. "HOLY CRAP, HOW THINGS HAVE CHANGED!!!!!"

I walk into the motor pool and see my ride. I can't help but feel it will either be my gold chariot to healing or my dark hearse back to hell. Either way, I know this is the only chance I will get, and I am eager to find out which ride is waiting for me once this is over. We ride in silence, no need for me to tell him where we're going, as John has given him all the particulars. Suddenly the silence surrounding me feels claustrophobic, closing in on my resolve so heavily that my lungs are screaming for air.

"Was it worth it???" I blurt into the silence.

"At first," he speaks quietly, not uncomfortable or surprised by my intrusion. He was expecting it. "Consequences, Miss Reggie, are the reward for our kind of justice. My consequences caused me to land in prison, and like I said, I was okay with that at first. But eventually, I realized that the justice I chose would never bring her back. I couldn't even bury her properly, and I know she wouldn't have wanted me to end up sitting in a cell while she is placed in the dirt. I will never forget how the rage consumed every fiber of my being when I saw her dead on the floor of that hotel room. I didn't go there intending to kill that bastard, just to get her away from him. But rage is as strong an emotion as love or hate; we can't control any of them."

While I wait for him to continue, the green light of the blinker flashes through the cab of the truck, the ping that accompanies it sounds shrill and intrusive.

"I really should have just busted him up so severely that his body would remind him every day that he is suffering because he killed the most wonderful woman that existed. But the sad reality is, I'm the only one who suffered. I guess that's justice, that's my Reward. I know what you feel you need to do, but know this: I will not let you go so far you end up where I did. Besides, there's a man at the Club House who would never forgive me if I did."

"You too? Am I the only one who didn't see John's feelings?" I ask, looking over at him. The only response I get is a noncommittal shrug of his huge shoulders, which pretty much answers my question.

We sit in silence again, his words soaking into my brain, and I suddenly feel comforted knowing he will have my back tonight. "Thank you, Mountain," I say, noticing my voice depicts a strength now that I should have had a long time ago. I look forward to the mental judgment to come after I deliver my own justice; the consequences will be welcome as I know they will be just.

Chapter 33

The house is dark as we pass by; it's 2:30 a.m., and the neighborhood is quiet. Benjamin should be asleep by now. Mountain finds a place to park at the curb a few houses down from Benjamin's. Suzie is getting antsy, placing her paw on my shoulder—it's like she is begging not to be left in the truck by herself. I give her a hug and tell her she is coming with us, that I need her and Mountain both.

"John had me put what you asked for in the back. I'll grab it for you." We both open our doors and close them as quietly as possible. "Here you go," Mountain whispers and hands me my bat. "Make him suffer, Miss Reggie." Again, I don't need to be analyzed or judged as I grab it almost lovingly. I can only imagine what a shrink would label this behavior, and again, I don't give a crap because it's my own kind of therapy. I'm not swinging at Benjamin Troy tonight—oh, it's his body, but I'll see a different face attached.

We head to Benjamin's house, the snow devouring the sounds of our footsteps as we leave the truck behind and head toward my long-past-due act of redemption. We slowly maneuver our way to the back of the house and quietly step onto the wooden porch. Mountain quietly bends down in front of the door and begins to pick the lock. I reach down and place my fingers and thumb softly around Suzie's muzzle, giving her our unique sign for silence and look into her eyes—she understands.

While I wait in the silence for Mountain to finish at the door, I look over and see an old Adirondack chair pushed up against the side of the house. I picture Clarissa sitting there holding a kitten to her chest lovingly, gently stroking its fur and whispering praise, but that was before Benjamin's jealousy destroyed the pure love and companionship she felt for the creature. Thinking of the cruelty to both her and the kitten only solidifies why this message will be delivered for both of us.

Mountain has gained entrance without a sound, and as I step through the door, I am immediately looking at Benjamin's safe. I know the surveillance camera is still in place, so I look up into the light fixture and give a nod. Mountain motions for me and Suzie to stay put while he finds and secures

Benjamin. After a few darkly shadowed minutes, we hear:

"What the hell!!!!" followed by a very loud, satisfying crunch. Then it sounds like furniture being moved followed by a few subtle grunts. The quick grating hiss of a zip tie rings through the quiet darkness before the tearing of a thick piece of duct tape is ripped off its roll and harshly slapped onto Benjamin's mouth, smothering his pathetic muttering.

Mountain appears shortly and whispers in my ear, "He may have a broken jaw. Don't know how that happened." I nod and move toward the bedroom as Mountain reaches over to place his hand on Suzie's back, indicating she is to stay with him.

I slip through the living room slowly and noiselessly as my eyes adjust to the darkness. Each step I take brings me closer to Benjamin's rage and the pain he feels from his broken jaw. I hear his muted cries of pain as bloody mucus flows from his nose to connect with the duct tape across his mouth. But the satisfaction I feel is weak; my mind wants more as it feeds the tingle I feel, reminding me it's only a taste of what's to come. I'm gripping my bat so tight with my right hand I know my knuckles must be white as they fill with icy payback. Every nerve in my body is gearing up for a satisfying delivery; the electrifying tingle jolting its spark rapidly through my limbs somehow leaves me strangely calm. I remind myself it doesn't matter whose face I see or whose body I will permanently destroy—this is for Clarissa and me. When I have delivered enough justice here tonight, both of us will be able to move forward. It's time for me to write a different ending to my story.

Chapter 34

When I step into the bedroom, the only light there is coming from a nightlight plugged into the wall next to the door. It will be easy for me to stay out of that small glow and Benjamin's view, which works perfectly in my favor. It's too dangerous for him to distinguish my features, so I'm wearing my hood pulled down as far as I can, hiding as much of my face as possible just in case he catches a glimpse somehow. I'm ready to be as evil as the creator that raised him; there will be no second-guessing my actions here tonight. My humanity cocktail pulses with a strong resolve in the morals blender, urging me to find peace on the other side of darkness.

"Your jaw must really hurt. Did you accidentally get hit by a shovel head? Oh no, wait, that was Clarissa!!! She sends her regards, by the way." He hisses behind the tape like the devil's baby he is, pulling on the arm that is zip-tied to the bedpost. He struggles and tries to spit his cruel demands through the tape—he still doesn't get the fact that he's not in control. I slowly place my bat on the bed and sit on the edge, very dramatically, feeling empowered and hoping there's enough light that he can see it. His eyes are stinging from salty tears as they roll downward, carrying the pain of his jaw, and the sight is enormously satisfying. Well done, Mountain!

"Benjamin, you can think of me as the Mistress of Darkness. I'm here to deliver a message from Clarissa." I let that sink in and watch him squirm as my voice filters through the darkness. "Before I'm done here tonight, there will be no doubt in your mind that I will do what I say, because I'm going to destroy your body and your connection to evil tonight! The Devil is going to see you as a failure and leave you to rot in the destroyed shell you call a body." He begins kicking into the dark room, trying to exact some power over the situation. So I wait until he's spent and begin again, but first, I pick up my bat and hold it lovingly. "Unlike the hidden coward you have always been, Benjamin, I'm going to tell you what's about to happen and why!" I stand now and lean in close, grabbing his jaw—I can feel and hear the unnatural movement and the grating sound of pain I'm causing. He bucks and convulses like the wounded pathetic specimen he is, so of course, I pinch harder. He tries to swing out with his unrestrained hand, but I quickly knock it back and step on his fingers when his hand hits the floor. I turn his face away from me and whisper in his ear, "This one's for Clarissa." I swing the bat back and bring it swooshing through the darkness and drop it solidly across his stomach. Air tries to funnel out of his mouth as it rides on a nasty gasp of agony, but it's blocked by the barrier of tape, and he has no choice but to choke on it, making me smile into the darkness. I stand back and watch the convulsions from my delivery and feel some vindication run through me. I don't allow him much time for recovery before I whisper, "And this one's for the nurse you left to bleed out in the parking lot of the hospital." I lift my arms and feel the weight I hold in my hand—I am in control now, so I swing again and hit the elbow of his arm that is extended up and tied to the bedpost. The sound is sick but satisfying, gruesome but beautiful—I am sinking deeper into my revenge. Yes, this is what I came here for.

At this point, he is screaming into the tape across his mouth and trying to sit up straighter to alleviate the pull on his arm. I am suddenly slapped with the smell of urine seeping into the carpet under him, the hot liquid spreading around his legs. Now he knows what it's like to seriously lose control and be terrified.

I am so keyed up at this point, I realize I'm riding a high that could easily destroy me again. I know instantly I could go too far. That realization brings back Mountain's words, and I am able to rein myself in. I gaze through the dimness of the room and watch his body language—even at this point, he won't back down. He pulls his knee back and begins to kick, and that's all I needed to carry on. "And Benjamin, this one's for me," I whisper with hatred and bring the bat back up over my shoulder. I bring it down with such force on his knee it is destroyed beyond recognition. I think he might have passed out, but am so oblivious to his pain I don't care. I begin to lose it into the bedroom and onto the lump of flesh on the floor as I scream at my past and the bastard who brought me here. Benjamin is just a means to an end for my revenge, an evil twin raised by the darkness. I have no more internal struggles to fight and no regrets as I continue. "No more will you control me, no more!!! I'm finally getting back every piece of me you took, slowly regaining who I was and what I wanted before you consumed me. I'm healing, getting stronger, you sadistic bastard. So pass that onto your dark creator when you see him in hell!!!"

I'm breathing heavily into the room as I try to control my actions and my need for redemption. But as Benjamin begins to stir, the little control I felt disappears into the bat, pushing the need to deliver just a little more pain. I swing the bat up one more time and bring it down on his exposed ankle. The way his foot lays awkwardly from the damaged joint makes me feel vindicated, but not thoroughly. I want to continue my cleansing by swinging again. I want to watch the seepage of his decay as it leaches from his pores and he screams for me to stop. I lift the bat one more time but feel a resistance. Looking up, I see Mountain's large hand holding it firmly at my shoulder. He leans in close and whispers, "You done good, Miss Reggie, you done good."

I suddenly lose every ounce of strength and need for revenge I had and let go of the bat as I fall into his chest, letting the horror that was once my life surge from me like the ripple of water through my fingers. He stands strong, circling me with his arms and whispering, "It's over now, girl, you can find yourself again." I hold on tight and sob as if every bit of me has been vindicated, as if my soul can now heal and my journey for the life I never had slowly begins to come into view.

As we stand facing each other in front of Benjamin, my stance is my own and strong, my life is my own, and the next breath I take will be clean and cleansing. I feel the forgiveness toward myself enter as a soft warmth spreading through my body. There's a soft flicker of light behind my eyes as they are being opened to a future—a future of my choice. My heart feels the glow and responds; the deadness it has felt for so long begins to pack its bags for retreat.

I turn in Mountain's arms and speak to Benjamin with a hatred I know I will never be able to let go of, but at the same time, I know it will never define me again. "If you ever go near Clarissa again, I'll be back. You still have one good knee, and as I've been told I need more batting practice, I guess I've been dropping my shoulder a bit. And know this, you soulless bastard, we will always be watching. There is no place you can hide and no place you can run that our eyes won't find you. There's no place you will ever be safe from us. So, with that being said, I suggest you watch this as soon as possible," I say and pull out a flash drive from the pocket of my jeans and throw it on the bed. "You might want to take a look at that before you get any ideas about talking."

Chapter 35

We no sooner pile ourselves into the cab of the truck when Mountain's phone lights up with an incoming message. "It's John," he says and begins dialing.

"Of course, it is," I say with a sense of comfort. "You did so good, Suzie, you are such a good girl," I say and hug her close. I hear Mountain speaking to John as he lets him know all is good and we're all safe. I take a deep breath and, looking down, my eyes catch the blood covering my bat. I can smell the strong scent of copper within the small confines of the cab. I can feel the sticky reminder of my actions on my hands and feel a sadness for the necessity of how we need to fight this never-ending war of abuse. I am in no way sorry or judgmental of myself for dispensing the same pain that was pushed onto so many victims, me included. Yes, my intent for payback was pushed, and my resolve to do it was strong as I wielded the punishment. We're not perpetuating a cycle of rage and abuse; we're fighting it by mirroring its actions. I stare at the blood and feel I have pounded at least two permanent nails into the lid of the well where my guilt still stirs, but it won't stir for long because I have earned the right to plead my internal and emotional case. But not tonight; my mind and body need to rest before I will know if the outcome of my actions tonight will set me free.

We enter the Club House through the motor pool as usual and make our way to the conference room where we will discuss the events of tonight and what will come next. John is pacing back and forth behind Michael and Abby, who are at one end of the table with Xander and Matt sitting on both sides. Mountain nods to everyone and takes a seat at the other end.

"How are you, Reggie?" Abby asks as I gingerly find my own chair and call Suzie close to me. The concern in her voice is as if she's asking a teenager about her first breakup, and I can't help but smile, saying I'm exhausted but feel strong. Her eyes brim with tears as she nods her head in understanding.

John makes his way over to my chair and takes one of my blood-covered hands; his eyes show concern, so I reach over with the other and place it on top of his. "This isn't mine," I refer to the dried, sticky mess covering them like a glove. "I have a feeling Benjamin isn't going to be any trouble. I delivered a dangerous and distinct message."

"But at what price?" John says with downcast eyes.

"The only price that matters!" I say strongly to everyone at the table as I squeeze his hand in assurance.

"She did good, Boss. That guy will never be able to watch another baseball game as long as he lives. She loves her batting practice," Mountain says with pride, which turns into a silent sadness that the whole room picks up on.

I suddenly feel so tired and dirty; I just want to shower and crawl into bed. Not crawl in and hide like usual—never again will I hide. I feel my emotional exile is coming to an end, and for the first time, I can't wait to see what tomorrow will bring. I can read the emotions on their faces and am encouraged by the love I see and feel from all of them. This is my family; this is what concern and trust are all about. I have come home.

"I'll see you all in the morning," I say with exhaustion. "I'll let Mountain fill you in on the particulars because I really need a shower and some sleep." I slowly stand and head for the door as everyone in the room nods in understanding. But before I walk out of the room, I stop beside Mountain, placing my hand on his shoulder—what, I initiated contact. "Thank you, Mountain, for everything, I really mean it," I say and begin to pull my hand away, but before I do, his huge, gentle hand finds mine and gives it a squeeze of understanding.

As I make my way to the Bunk House with Suzie, the emotional tsunami of relief and freedom begins crashing against the barriers I have hidden behind for so long. Each barrier holds a different tortured inlet of abuse, making up a natural harbor of fear and shame. Each one begins to crumble before my eyes, sending the multiple degrees of degradation out to sea on an angry wave. My emotions are rapidly swirling and dancing among the waves in celebration of my newfound freedom. The celebrating will continue in earnest until my emotions are drunk with a sense of vindication and peace. They relish the idea of my past being set afloat on a burning vessel. There will be no captain to guide its darkness, no engineer to put out the flames; it will float for eternity in a cold purgatory of evil.

I watch the blood drip from my fingers as I stand under the hot spray of the shower, the water pushing it to the drain where it disappears out of sight. Everything feels different now; everything looks different now. I reach out and place my hand on the decorative tile lining the shower stall, thinking I never noticed the colors before. I start laughing softly to myself and place my forehead against the tile, wondering about all the changes to come and what else I haven't noticed.

Once I'm done in the bathroom, I make my way to our bunk where Miss Suzie has already begun to warm up the blankets for our slumber. She eyes me lovingly and lifts her head as I slip under the blankets and sigh with comfort. She places her head on my chest, and we both begin to slip into sleep. Suddenly, I feel a weight on the other side of the bed and hear John say, "Scoot over some, girls, I need more room." Without a word, Suzie and I do as we're told. I hear John's boots hit the floor and feel his warmth as he lays down on top of the covers beside me.

It's as if we've been doing this for years—it's natural and special and pure; it's heaven. I readjust myself and lay my head on his muscled chest. "I'm glad you see me," I say into the soft light of the room.

His strong arm claims me and pulls me close, as he places a light kiss on the top of my head. His chest begins to rumble under my ear, and he says, "We're definitely going to need a bigger bed."

Chapter 36

I push my way through the huge, imposing doors of my mythical trial and make my way to the defense table. Today, I am expected to justify my actions and explain the stain and strain on my morals and obscured humanity. This court will get the facts that caused my low character, not excuses for it. Once they have that information, I'm hopeful that they will understand why I chose the manner of exorcism I did to excise my malignant tumor of guilt. But no matter what transpires as I sit to be judged, there will be no throwing myself on the mercy of this imaginary court, and there will be no deals. I look around and see I'm the only one here so far, so I take a seat and wait—wait for what I hope is the day I get the verdict I need and deserve. Today, I hope I will be told to pound the rest of the nails into the cover of the well where my guilt resides. Today is the day I find out if I can be a SURVIVOR!

I hear a door open and close somewhere in the room. I look over and see the Prosecutor floating to the table next to me, and I know him instantly. Benjamin's creator has decided to prosecute my actions himself. He has only one witness, and that's Benjamin, who is trying to sit at the table, but because his body is so beautifully grotesque and bloody, he is finding it hard to do so. As satisfied as I am to see his difficulty, I suddenly wonder if I have made a mistake as to the meaning of this hearing.

"All rise," we hear from the faceless entity at the front of the courtroom, "this court is called to order." Then suddenly, another faceless entity appears and is sitting behind the imposing bench at the front of the room. The sound of a gavel making a loud crack as it connects with whatever it is gavels connect with, and we are told to be seated.

"Good evening, people. I am sorry we have to meet to discuss these distasteful events, but there have been a number of distasteful events this evening, and I need to hear the facts. Ms. Reynolds, I assume you have witnesses here tonight to testify on your behalf."

"Yes, your Honor," I say and turn to the back of the room where all my emotions have settled in and are ready to vindicate my actions.

"Excellent!"

"Objection, your Honor," we hear from the prosecution table where the Devil is suddenly standing before the court. He's a menacing creature and uses intimidation, even here, to try and portray superiority over the courtroom. He's as deranged and evil above ground as he is below, where he wallows in the molten lava he calls home. He feels his mere presence will intimidate, sending the judge and the rest of us running while he holds his dark staff in his hand and swishes his nasty tail like a petulant child.

"To what, Counselor???" the Judge snaps in irritation. "We haven't even started yet, so I suggest you sit down and retract those horns and manage that tail of yours in my courtroom!"

"Now, I am here to determine if Ms. Reynolds acted morally and justly this evening. I need to hear all the evidence her witnesses can provide. I need to listen to all the facts pertaining to her prior years of abuse—all the facts pertaining to why she carries a strong sense of guilt, especially since she was left disfigured like that," he says and points to me with what I can only describe as sadness. "She has the right to vindicate her actions, and I have a duty to make a determination if she will be set free from her guilt."

"Ms. Reynolds, are you ready to proceed? Are you ready to plead your case to this court?"

"Yes and no, your Honor!" I state strongly. "I will call witnesses to describe the reasons for my actions, but not to make excuses for them. I will not waste the court's time because I don't feel the need to justify my extreme actions to an inhuman injustice."

"Again, your Honor, I object to the way she addressed this court and you, sir!"

"Very noble of you, Counselor, but I can take care of myself. And don't think for a minute that this little display of kissing my ass will get you into my good graces! Now sit down!"

"But your Honor, look what she did to my client!"

"I have eyes in my head, Counselor. Now shut the hell up and let's get on with this!"

"Ms. Reynolds, before you call your witnesses, I have a few questions. Stand before this court, please."

"Yes, your Honor," I say and stand on strong, determined legs.

"Do you regret your actions?"

"The only regret I have is the reality we live in, the reality that left me no choice if I wanted to be free."

"I see, but why did you think beating the crap out of this disgusting creature would rid you of your guilt?"

"Again, your Honor, I object to your reference of my client as disgusting!"

"Seriously!!! He wouldn't look like that if not for you; you're lucky you aren't the one on trial here today!!! Your objection is overruled!"

"Your Honor, I felt the need to punish that man," I say and point at Benjamin, "in that manner because he is one of the Prosecutor's demented soldiers. I needed to abuse him in order to vindicate Clarissa's life of pain. He was just a stand-in for all the other soldiers the Prosecutor has marching around out there that we will never be able to stop because it will always be too late. I wanted him to be an example to all the others; I wanted to let them know that if we catch up with them, this is what to expect! And yes, I had a selfish reason also. Truth be told, your Honor, he was the replacement I needed to destroy in order to end my guilt for good."

As he looks away from me, a bantering between counsel and the court begins again, leaving me to have a clear eye-opening epiphany. I am standing here in front of the entire courtroom of onlookers and suddenly realize I don't need their absolution or favorable verdict of my actions. All I need is to let go of my past, let go of the pain, and now I know I am ready to do that on my own. I can finally see that living with my scars is nothing compared to living day in and day out with a heavy, unwarranted coat of guilt. I finally realize that the guilt is just another method for him to control me, even from the grave. Well, who has the last laugh now? I say to myself and proceed to hammer in two more nails while cc-ing my guilt a copy of my epiphany.

"Ms. Reynolds, please call your first witness."

As I am pulled back from my thoughts, I proceed. One by one, my familiar emotions—Fear, Domination, Shame, Pain, Degradation, Intimidation, Humiliation, and Misery—take the stand and begin to read from the chapters of my dark novel. Each one paints a picture with their words in order to bring a visual portrait of my past life into view. Each one describes their personal knowledge and insight into an intricate darkness. As they continue one by one to lay out my past within the courtroom, I stand tall, and with each passing minute, I allow myself to confront each piece, each memory head-on for the last time. I find myself able to say goodbye with a certainty they will never return. I feel lighter now that my story is out there; I feel there will never again be a reason for me to hide, for me to tremble through the night. But at the same time, I have no delusions—there will be triggers, my personal form of PTSD, along the way. Triggers that will send me back to one chapter or another of my story because they remind me of a horror. But I have the strength now to cope with the past, and I don't need amnesty or a pardon from this court to pound the last few nails into the lid of that well and forget what lurks beneath it forever. I will walk out of this courtroom with my head held high and a strong will to fight for the future I deserve.

The gavel comes down again, sending finality to these proceedings. I don't wait for the verdict; suddenly, I turn and walk the carpeted path to the doors of the courtroom. I don't care what comes next; I do not need to hear the decision because it doesn't matter—I have done it, I have figured it out on my own. I push through the doors and glance back before they close, shutting off my past. I allow myself to enjoy the satisfaction of what I see—or rather don't see—judgment will not be passed on me today. The room will hold my secrets in silence; it will fill the empty space with a sorrowful understanding as to my actions.

Chapter 37

My eyes pop open when I feel the bed shift and see John bending over to put his boots on. He stands and gestures for Suzie to follow, so she picks up her baby and jumps off the bed—the little traitor. I smile sleepily as they leave and roll over, pulling the covers tight around me, and am surprised by the relief and comfort that simple gesture gives me—I'm relaxed. As I lay in this bed, cocooned among the blankets, my mind is clear, not clouded by defeat any longer. I regard my new reality as a do-over, in some respects. Every piece of me was stolen; everything I wanted to achieve has been wiped out by a predator. I know in my heart I will never find the me I should have been—too much time has passed. But I can find a new me, a different me, one that I can respect and grow with. I will leave the me that could have been behind, just like my past. I will forget the normalcy that should have been and find a normalcy for the future. I will stop missing what I never had or achieved because a different future awaits me now, and he just walked out the door.

My dream starts to filter into my mind in bits and pieces, and for the first time, I want to remember all of it. I giggle when I wonder what that absurd trial's outcome would have been. I wonder if the holes in my soul formed by my low morals and damaged humanity had any impact, whether they made a positive or negative difference on the verdict. I think about all the emotions that had controlled me for so long; I think about how I confronted each and every one of them even though they helped me plead my case. I will take my hodgepodge of emotions and form them into a haphazard pattern. I will fit them together to complete my history—an emotional quilt of my past. Every quilt has an origin; it is designed by a certain time and place, and its meaning is described by shapes and colors. My quilt pieces are dark and sad, full of painful memories, but also strength. With them, I will find an untapped strength in which to wrap myself heavily and move forward. Over time, the pieces will begin to fray and fade as I continually swaddle myself up tight and relish in the knowledge they didn't beat me. Instead, they will help me to find the woman I will become! They've already pointed me in the right direction!

I hear a knock on the door, and when I roll over, I see Clarissa standing there.

"Hey, you," I say and sit up, "how's it goin'?"

"I wanted to thank you. I heard some of what you did for me last night and am so grateful."

I look at her and say, "As strange as this may sound, what I did last night wasn't just for you—it was for me as well."

"I think I understand," she says, "I hope it helped!"

"It did!"

"Well, John asked me to come and get you. He wants us all in the conference room. Something about clippers and Oscar-D," she gestures with her hands in the air, confused. "Oh, and something about duct tape was mentioned."

"Okay," I say with a laugh. "I'll be there in a bit."

I head to the conference room and can hear the excitement and yelling before I even make it to the door. Looking inside, I see John trying to wrestle Oscar-D toward a chair while Dominic struggles to get ahold of an arm to duct tape it to the chair.

"Oh, come on, Boss!!! You're not really going to do this, are you?" Oscar-D screams while fidgeting in the chair.

"Nope, I'm not doing the honors. Dominic paid me to let him lead this mission. Or should I say, The Dominator paid me."

It is standing room only by the time the clippers are plugged in and the chair of shame, with Oscar-D strapped in tight, is rolled into position. As the struggling in the chair continues, Dom begins his taunting dance with animated glee. He bends down and sends a sinister laugh into Oscar-D's face, turning the clippers on and off for effect while smiling like the Joker who has Batman in a dire situation.

"Oh, come on, Dominator, you're my bro, bro!"

"I paid good money for this action, bro, and you deserve it, bro! A deal's a deal!" And with that, the first swipe of the clippers takes out a chunk of hair consisting of two large dreads, and the whimpering begins. Manly whimpering, but whimpering all the same. The background noise is exaggerated, as hysterical animation erupts from team members who start making bets. The big-money bets are on whether he will or won't cry before it's over. I hear someone yell from the crowd and realize it's Abby. She's laughing so hard but manages to wave a $100 bill in the air, betting that he'll definitely cry.

"Seriously????? Oh, come on, Momma, that's just cruel!!!"

I make my way over to stand by John as the antics continue. It's so good to see everyone smiling and letting their guard down, even if it is just for a little while. John puts his arm around me and pulls me close; it is so natural we didn't even look at each other to acknowledge the newness of the act. I feel like I have come home after a long absence and am smoothly picking up with a life I left behind.

I tell John I'm going to see how Pix is doing—I can't watch this sad end to the dreads any longer. Besides, I find I feel sorry for Oscar-D on some kind of weird level. But I also know that kid will get himself into a situation like this again, so I won't waste too much time feeling sorry for him. He will spend enough time regretting his actions on his own. Every time he looks in the mirror and runs his hands over the bald beacon atop his shoulders, he will feel and see the consequence of his impatient impulse. And as I walk through the door, I smile to myself when I hear someone call out, "Chrome Dome."

I make my way through the doors of the Medical Bay and am greeted by Janet, the nurse attending to Pix this morning. She says to go right in—that she was just with Pix and she's awake. I glance at Suzie, who has followed me in, and then look at Janet. "She's fine; she can go in," I'm told.

"Thank you, come on, Suz." I walk to the back of the room where the cloth partition is pulled around the bed to give some privacy. I peek around the end of the curtain and say hi, while Suzie does her own brand of peeking into the space. I see Pix lying in the hospital bed looking even smaller than usual, no bigger than a sick child. Her arms are covered in gauze and bandages; a translucent tube feeds her liquids from an IV bag hanging from a metal pole to her left. Her face is pale from all the blood loss she sustained, and her blue eyes are hooded by heavy eyelids, but she manages a tired smile.

"What's going on out there?" Pix asks as I enter. "Sounds like I'm missing one hell of a party!" But before I can reply, Pix holds out her hand—the one not hooked up to an IV—and touches Suzie's head. "Hi, sweet girl." As usual, Suzie leans into the touch and tries to pull all the pain from Pix. It makes no difference if the pain is physical or mental, because that's her job.

"You are. Oscar-D is fighting the deal he made about shaving his head—the poor kid. When I left, he didn't have too many dreads left. Unfortunately, with that kid, having the biggest heart on the planet also means having no patience and a big mouth," I say, laughing.

Pix looks at me with a foggy stare induced by pain meds. "You look different," she says while trying to adjust herself into a comfortable position.

"I feel different," I say, acknowledging her observation. "How are you feeling?"

"Xander forgets I'm a nurse, and I really don't need all these IV fluids he's got me hooked up to. Besides, they just make me have to pee every fifteen minutes. I should be up and walking a bit by now!!!" she screams out to Janet through the curtain.

"What's that, Pix? Did you say you want an enema???" Janet responds.

"Nope, sure didn't, Janet, but thanks so much for asking!"

"Then zip it!!!"

At this point, all Pix can do is roll her eyes in defeat.

"Hey, it's been less than 24 hours; don't push it!"

She tries to roll over onto her uninjured side and grimaces with pain as she moves. My respect for her is suddenly overwhelming, and my hope that she will stay with the team is important to me.

"So, it went well last night? Clarissa is safe?"

"Yes, she's definitely safe for the near future. We'll always be watching him, and her, of course! Pix, I'm curious where your thoughts are about Mickey at this point. Do you think you'll stay with us?"

She pulls in a long breath and looks at something in the room that only she can see before she answers. "I've been thinking a lot about that, even though it's through the drug fog, but I want to stay. I believe in this team and what we can do. Our ability to help before it's too late can make a difference to women who are trapped in a no-win scenario. I know we can't end this madness, but we can make a difference on a small scale, one case at a time."

I knew the look she wore well. She was traveling back from her own story, being chased by memories and regret. But suddenly she looks at me and shuts down the pain, turning the last page and closing the book on her story.

"So, what's next for Clarissa?"

"She will start over somewhere with a new identity, begin a new life. If Clarissa gives the okay, you can get the particulars from Abby. For me, this is as far as I go with Clarissa, besides wishing her well, of course. The way I deal with this job is to keep a distance from our rescues once they are safe. That's all I care about—making sure they're safe. And I can do that because I know our team will watch over them for as long as it's needed." I step over and touch her hand softly. "You need your rest now. I'll see you later. Maybe we can get permission to take you for a short walk."

I turn to leave and see I'm not the only visitor Pix will have this morning. Matt is standing outside the curtain with a bouquet of flowers in hand and a shy smile plastered on his face. Suddenly, it hits me that Matt is the one who should help Pix take a walk. I make a mental note to talk to John, to see if he knows how Matt is handling things before we find ourselves right back in the middle of a case. I need to know his head is on straight, for the safety of everyone, including him.

Chapter 38

Three days after Pix was stabbed, she joined me and Suzie to say our goodbyes to Clarissa. Matt has pushed her wheelchair out to the gate next to the airfield, making sure she was warm enough by placing a blanket across her lap and smiling shyly as he did so. Apparently, he hasn't left her side since the stabbing. On some level, we know he feels guilty for not getting there in time to stop the brutal act, but I can see Pix is helping him with that. Not just her understanding of how he feels, but by being alive and continuing to recover, that will make all the difference to his own recovery. He will be fine—well, as fine as any of us can be with the job we have chosen to do, with the life we have been called into because we're needed in the worst way.

John has filed the flight plan and is ready to whisk Clarissa off to her new life. It is 9:00 p.m., and the runway is slick with a fresh coat of snow, and the darkness is weakened with the lights of the runway every few feet. We are standing close enough to the warehouse that the security lights affixed to the roof give us enough light for our goodbyes. Clarissa gives each of us an individual hug of thanks and gratitude, leaving the need for words unnecessary—no words were expected anyway; the action said it all.

As John makes his way out of the Club House, Matt turns Pix around and heads back in, passing him on the way. John says something over his shoulder, and Pix laughs into the cold night.

"You wish, Boss!"

When he reaches us, he leans in close to me and whispers, "I'll see you tomorrow."

"Be safe," I respond and hug him tight. He kneels down and gets his kiss from Suzie, her actions saying the same thing: be safe.

As he stands, he looks at us and smiles, "You two stay out of trouble now!" Suzie responds for both of us with a snort and a high-pitched bark, which mirrored my sentiments exactly.

All I knew about Clarissa's journey was that she would be joining her mother at an exclusive and very private nursing home facility. One of our many hidden companies had filtered money through one of our many LLCs to purchase it. The ownership is hidden behind so many different entities it would be almost impossible to track it. But "almost" poses as much of a threat as slapping our name on the front door and telling Benjamin Clarissa is there, so a team will always be on site for further protection. Clarissa will be housed in a small adjoining cottage on its grounds where she will be close to her mother. What she will do after her mother passes will be up to her, but she knows we will give her the means with which to do it.

John leads Clarissa out to the safety of the plane, and when they are at the foot of the stairs, Suzie and I watch them ascend to the top and step through the open door. Once they are inside, the stairs are slowly lifted up and secured tightly. This is where Clarissa will leave her old existence behind and hopefully be able to be happy. I wait for the chance to see John look out the small window of the cockpit but realize how silly that is due to the darkness and the distance between us.

As Suzie and I stand there being pelted softly with new snow, watching Mickey's plane taxi down the runway, I can't help but revel in my well-earned freedom. The snow coming down covers all the past I have carried around for so long, and when it melts, everything will be new and clean, just like my future. I have finally found my closure thanks to Clarissa's case and Benjamin, AKA, "Him!!!"

The plane's engines fire up, and it begins to push forward, slowly at first, but then gains speed as it travels down the runway. The lights on the wings eventually lift slowly from the ground as if being levitated into the dark sky by magic. Suzie lets forth a small bark and looks up at me, leaving me to suddenly realize I will miss the man piloting the plane, even if he'll only be gone for one night. There's so much to look forward to and experience moving forward. I think back on all the years wasted when I didn't even allow myself to think about moving forward, to think I didn't deserve anything close to happiness. I have found my family among the team of Mickey. The camaraderie is special, solidified by our chosen profession and the unwavering need to fight against an enemy who can't be stopped. All we can do is help one victim at a time. I am so grateful and overwhelmed to know I have John and his parents—it's unexpected and extraordinary, to say the least.

The snow continues to fall, but I have no intention of going back inside. I want to watch the lights of the plane fade, leaving only darkness to envelop the two individuals inside. Small, purifying flakes of white begin to stick to my emotional quilt, which hangs off my shoulders. The fading and fraying process has begun; the dampness is setting in—it won't be long now. As each flake connects, I can hear their promise and encouragement to wait just a bit longer. Their acknowledgment of the pain of my past is slowly slipping away in order for me to move forward, because I have journeyed far enough under the darkness. I spread my arms out from my body and take a deep breath. Closing my eyes, I lift my head up to the blackened sky and begin to twirl around in place. I feel the soggy remains of my emotional quilt begin to slowly drip off my arms, free falling soundlessly to land harshly on the ground. They begin to disappear without a fight as they connect with the cold ground cover. As I continue to spin faster and faster, their existence disappears into cold slush beneath my boots. I stop spinning once every piece of the faded and frayed quilt has disappeared from my arms. Silently, I acknowledge to no one and everyone, that now I can be called: "A SURVIVOR!!!"

Epilogue

The Present

It's been strangely quiet since we wrapped up Clarissa's case, and there have been many adjustments confronted between John and me—oh, and Suzie, of course. When John returned from delivering Clarissa to the beginning of her new life, we became inseparable and totally comfortable with the new direction we knew our lives were taking. We spent many hours discussing procedures while we lay together at night in our bigger bed. We both agreed it was still the wisest plan for me to take the rescues to a motel the first night of extraction. That has always been for the protection of everyone, and that shouldn't change just because John and I are now together.

The day after John returned from delivering Clarissa to her new life, he hired a couple of contractors to wall off the other end of the Bunk House. It was a mirror image of the private guest room the rescues are housed in when they begin their transition. We are taking it slow and haven't even talked about the future—he doesn't want to move too fast, and I am grateful. However, Abby and Michael have an entirely different opinion about where we should live, and that's with them, of course.

Suzie is taking all the changes in stride as John and I become closer. She knows that we have come so far and shared so much that she will never be replaced in my heart, and I know the same.

Pix is doing well. In fact, I can see her slowly walking laps up on the track, and of course, her constant companion is with her. Matt is giving her encouragement and making her laugh nonstop. Xander says just a few more days' observation, and she can go home, but not back to work for at least three more weeks. Michael has made all the arrangements with the hospital for her leave—her job will be there for her once she is released and can resume her duties.

As for Oscar-D, he is handling his baldness very well. He discovered there are weird people who shop on eBay looking for previously owned dreadlocks. Seriously, who knew? He has sold all of them but one—that one he keeps close, tied to his belt as a reminder of what his actions have cost him. At this point, he hasn't decided if he is going to grow his hair back or not; I guess we'll have to wait and see. I mean, Samson's long hair gave him immortal strength; maybe baldness will give Oscar-D some restraint, but then again, it's doubtful. God, I love the kid.

We have been lucky for a few days now and haven't been alerted to a case that needs our attention, so I thought it was a perfect time to follow up on the schooling John promised me concerning the batting cage. I am finally going to find out if he has game or just a big mouth. At first, I thought I would keep this demonstration private, just between us, but the more I thought about it, I just couldn't. My bad!

I sent out a blanket email to all the staff saying that if they could spare a little time, I would like them to grab a chair and plant themselves outside the batting cage. I promised them a show they would enjoy but didn't give any details of what to expect. I knew John would be walking through the door any minute as I was notified, per my request, that the plane had landed. He had filed a flight plan indicating he would be back and landing about 4:00

p.m. after having a meeting with a new Security Executive. He was always making sure we had the best equipment available. I had let Oscar-D in on my plan—I thought he deserved at least a little bit of payback. So, when John entered the Club House, Oscar-D was there to greet him and lead him to the batting cage where an audience of his peers was waiting. His look bore into me saying: you have got to be kidding me, when he saw me standing there with my bat in one hand and helmet in the other. All I could do is smile.

"Oh good, you're back!" I said with an animated squeal. Seriously, I actually squealed. "Ladies and gentlemen, I have been told by our leader here that he can hit a softball better than me. However, I feel that's highly doubtful, so I thought it was about time he put his money where his mouth is. How about it, John, are you ready to 'school me,' as you put it?"

The onlookers were catching on and began a rousing chant of: "BOSS, BOSS, BOSS!"

He decided to take me on, so when he started toward me, I nodded to Oscar-D, who hit a play button on his phone and John Fogerty's "Centerfield" began to play. "One of us will have a laugh when this is over," he whispered in my ear while taking the bat and helmet from my hands.

I walked him into the cage and started to explain how to adjust the settings, suggesting he take a few warm-up swings. "I can slow it down for you, big guy, if you want." I just couldn't resist that—again, my bad.

"Out," he says and points to the opening.

I do as I'm told and make my way out to the crowd of friends and family. He takes a few warm-up swings behind the plate before he hits the button on the pitching machine to program the speed of the pitch. Finally, he stands up to the plate and hits the button to receive the first pitch and waits. The ball comes right down the line to cross the strike zone, and he "SWINGS!!!!!"

WOW, I don't really know what I was expecting, but it definitely wasn't that.

THE END

Milton Keynes UK
Ingram Content Group UK Ltd.
UKHW021244191124
451300UK00007B/225